Praise for *All*

"Sharos takes us behind the curtain of the Advanced Placement exam and, in doing so, outlines some impactful strategies to maximize scores and learning. All Advanced Placement teachers will find a kindred spirit in the wisdom and stories Sharos provides throughout the book. This book is filled with hope, and it showcases how the intensity of AP learning is filled with relationships and life lessons that last much longer than the knowledge gained in the classroom."

—**Dr. Robert Dillon**, author, consultant, and director of innovation, University City School District

"'If you want to learn how to teach, then just teach.' Sage words of advice handed on from one generation of teachers to another. Here it is again, shared for a new era by Andrew Sharos. Straight from the shoulder, devoid of annoying academic jargon, searingly honest about failures and successes—Sharos gives us more than he imagines. Student outcomes are about students—not outcomes. Student success comes from discipline and interaction with a caring and demanding teacher. Student success can be pivotal and life changing. This is a good book. Heed its common-sense advice."

—**Steven M. Avella**, author, history professor, Marquette University

"Educators always look for inspiration and something to rejuvenate their spirit. Sharos's book provides practical best practices that can be implemented immediately in our AP classes. And his heartwarming stories of being one team in the AP classroom encourage me to remind my students we are in this game together. We will succeed!"

—**Malia Kau**, college counselor, Radford High School

"I appreciate the emphasis on relationships throughout the book. It includes tons of logical and practical pieces of advice, but it always comes back to the kids and their experiences. The influence of Sharos's own experiences as an AP student and his connections with other educators contribute to building a really authentic read."

—**Dr. Tony Sinanis**, award-winning principal, superintendent, and author of *Hacking Leadership*

"It should come as no surprise that this book moves beyond tips and tricks of student AP scores and gets at the very heart of what all our kids need: human support. Sharos beautifully outlines realistic strategies and the relationship needs that cannot be ignored in any AP classroom. You will find the softer side of Sharos's experience in the student success stories woven throughout this book of actionable AP advice. You'll see the connections and opportunities released when we believe in students and come to understand the reality that, without unwavering expectations, we do our students a great disservice."

—**Jenna Shaw,** educator and entrepreneur

"This is the AP book I have been waiting for! From the first chapter to the end, it is full of practical, applicable, and creative strategies. It does not contain complex theory, complicated data, pretense, or a one-size-fits-all approach to teaching. Sharos explains the idea that class culture matters, as does the us-against-the-test approach, which helps students succeed academically while adding value to each student and what they can contribute for the greater good. Another idea he shares—that hard work can be fun—is long overdue in the complexity of education today. Finally, it's a book that promotes building relationships as the key to student success. Thank you, Andrew, for your commitment to promoting hope!"

—**Edwina Henslee,** director, College Board

Andrew Sharos

A Guide to Teaching and Leading
Advanced Placement Programs

Published by Dave Burgess Consulting, Inc.
San Diego, CA
DaveBurgessConsulting.com

Cover Design by Genesis Kohler
Editing and Interior Design by My Writers' Connection

Library of Congress Control Number: 2018933187
Paperback ISBN: 978-1-946444-65-3
Ebook ISBN: 978-1-946444-66-0

First Printing: March 2018

CONTENTS

FOREWORD

This book embraces a very particular philosophy: *Every* student can do challenging academic work and be successful if they are properly supported.

When you begin to believe in this philosophy, there are some very specific effects. It makes you strive to explain, and then solve, the problems your students have. It makes *you* the most important element in getting students to achieve more. Whatever you do in a school, you owe it to yourself and the students you serve to examine this philosophy more closely. And this book is a great place to start.

Andrew Sharos started his teaching career like many of us did; he had drive and some content knowledge, but he had just a passing relationship with the art of teaching. However, every year he became better, and then came his call to action: He became the Advanced Placement United States History teacher at West Leyden High School. The class was difficult to teach. The students at our high school scored below average on standardized tests. An enormous percentage of them experience poverty at home. Lots of them don't know where their next meal is coming from. Many of them have jobs, and most of them carry responsibilities and experiences that kids their age simply shouldn't have.

It was in this context that Andrew became responsible for teaching a very difficult class. And he more than succeeded. *All* his students passed the Advanced Placement test, something that had not been done before in any subject on any test.

He achieved this remarkable feat by embracing the philosophy that *every* student can be successful at mastering difficult academic work and developing a set of useful, concrete practices that helped all his students learn effectively. Here is the book that explains how you can do the same. It's not easy, but it might be the most rewarding experience you can have in education.

This book is a very honest one. Andrew does not pretend that he taught with some special gift. The moments he shares about forming his ideas around teaching are heartfelt and sometimes painful. I was there to witness many of them, and they are how he describes them. But it was what he learned from his experiences that led him to achieve great things. We're lucky that he's now sharing those experiences with us.

Andrew's drive is infectious. If you have ever wished that you worked alongside a colleague who was always full of good ideas and enthusiasm, now you have exactly that. Take this book with you back to your classroom, office, or wherever you influence young people's lives and dive into it whenever you need good advice or a lift to your spirits.

Spoiler alert! The underdogs in this story win. The kids learn more about themselves and history than anyone could ever dream of. Our hero pulls off the impossible and lives to tell the tale. But read their story even though you know the ending. It's a great one, and I promise you that you will change your outlook on education, kids, teachers, and what it means to believe that every kid can achieve great things if they are supported properly.

Because every kid can. Let Andrew Sharos show you how.

Andrew Grieve
English Teacher, West Leyden High School

INTRODUCTION

This is a book about teaching and leading.

It is not like the ones you've read before as part of professional development, graduate school, or a book study. You won't find research-based methodology or throngs of data attached to any of my assertions. You will find practical ideas and inspiration coming from one educator to another.

If I were to ask you, "What is your greatest accomplishment as an educator?" do you know which story you would tell?

I stood in the hallway outside the social studies classrooms talking to my mentor-teacher. The district assigned him to the role four years prior when I began, and we had become good friends. He was everything I wanted to be as a teacher. All the faculty members respected him, he made teaching look easy, and the kids cemented him as a legend on our staff.

On this day, he chose to pass the torch, not because I earned it or because I was ready—and certainly not because I was all of the things he had become.

"I'm taking a professorship at Loyola University," he said. "Our department chair thinks you should take over my schedule and teach the AP classes. You got this."

This is where my story begins.

I spent the summer preparing to teach Advanced Placement United States History, or APUSH for short. I stopped coaching basketball to concentrate on this class. I started reading the textbook. I began copying as many of his files as I could. I scripted out my first two weeks of the class, in addition to planning for the other two "preps" I was assigned. Before I knew it, August arrived.

AP tests are graded on a 5-point scale, and a score of 4 or 5 virtually guarantees a student college credit at any university. Thankfully, expectations were not high, despite teaching the pantheon of classes in the department. The average AP score at our school was a 2.7 out of 5, and pass rates were below the national average. I knew I was teaching one of the toughest classes the AP offers. With just a 50 percent national pass rate, APUSH was a feared class for juniors around the country. During the previous year, students at our school scored a 1.96 class average and had an 18 percent pass rate on APUSH alone.

There were other challenges. We did not have an academic culture. Our school ACT average score barely crossed 18, well below state and national means. A 70 percent free- and reduced-lunch population added more intrigue to the obstacles our kids faced. There were some gangs, a mostly disengaged parent base, students who had to babysit their siblings, and some kids who worked just to keep the family financially afloat. Our district had an 80 percent Latino population, many of whom were first generation immigrants trying to provide a better life for their children. We described ourselves as a blue-collar community, and we took pride in that.

Does this sound familiar? Am I hitting some checkboxes of those you teach as well?

That is the last you will hear about school-wide obstacles in this book. I include them right away to frame the story. I couldn't write about our success if I taught at a ritzy high school and my students all had supportive homes, guaranteed meals, and private tutors.

The truth is, whatever success we had in the classroom can be attributed to that same group of students I just described.

What if I told you that after the first year of AP US History, our students scored a remarkable 3.87 average on the national exam? We had a 92 percent pass rate, a score the principal acknowledged as the highest class average in the history of the school.

What if I told you that after the second year, our students scored a class average of 4.37, and every single one of my students passed the exam? I was nominated for History Teacher of the Year. One of my students was subsequently invited to the White House to meet the president and speak about closing the Latino achievement gap.

And what if I told you that after the third year, every student who took the exam received a 4 or 5, giving us another 100 percent pass rate and the highest class average in the state of Illinois? That year our class average was 4.45 and College Board recognized our school as its "National District of the Year."

Would you believe me?

Or better yet, would you ask, "How?"

The ideas, methods, and stories that follow provide a guide to answering "how."

TRUE OWNERSHIP STARTS WITH A GIANT MIRROR

I sat in the back of the room with a scantron and an eighty-question multiple choice test in front of me like it was 1999 all over again. My forearms stuck to my desk as the ninety-degree September heat seeped into our classroom. In front of me sat twenty-eight of our students, nervously attempting their first test and wondering why their teacher was seated behind them as they tried to concentrate on the first question.

1. The headright system adopted in the Virginia Colony

   A) determined the eligibility of a settler for voting and hold-ing office.

   B) toughened the laws applying to indentured servants.

   C) gave 50 acres of land to anyone who would transport himself to the colony.

   D) encouraged the development of urban centers.

   E) prohibited the settlement of single men and women in the colony.

Whew. I knew the answer was C. I filled in the bubble on the scantron and moved to the next question. A few minutes later, a security guard named Frank entered the classroom with a pass for a student. He looked around the room trying to find me in the logical spots. We finally locked eyes, and he gave me an odd look as if to say, "What are ya doing back there?"

I will admit I sort of looked like Buddy the Elf squeezing my 6'4" frame into a high school desk.

This was the first time I was not sitting at my own desk grading papers or checking my email on test day. I will also admit I have given tests to my students without actually previewing every question. I may or may not have just printed off the answer key and used the electronic grading machine when it was all over. I ran the scantrons through the machine and emailed the class the results. The class average was 47 out of 80, good enough to be in play for a 3 on the AP exam but an F in the gradebook. Their average was aided by the performance of their teacher, who scored a respectable, but far from exemplary, 67/80.

By taking the exams with the students, I hoped to prove my support for them and that I was still learning too. We could review the exams together and talk aloud about which responses were deliberate distractors and how we arrived at correct answers. Our students could revel in the fact that they would sometimes answer a question correctly when their teacher answered wrong.

The first step in building empathy is putting yourself in someone else's shoes. This activity certainly afforded me that opportunity.

> ## The first step in building empathy is putting yourself in someone else's shoes.

Learning about my Advanced Placement teaching assignment thrust me into the role of leadership in my classroom and my department. Despite entering my fifth year of teaching, I was still one of the youngest members of our faculty, and I was teaching one of the only two AP classes the department offered. Naturally, I felt pressure to perform, knowing I would be under the watchful eye of my department colleagues, chairman, and the administration.

I cut my teeth as an educator teaching our lowest level of US history and was a member of the curriculum team. We had four members on our team with more than twenty years' experience individually, so I kept my eyes open and my mouth shut in meetings.

Back in my classroom, where I could be the expert, I told the stories of our nation's past with enthusiasm and passion. Many times during those first few years, however, I received feedback from colleagues about things I was doing and saying wrong in class. One teacher would sit in our office next to my classroom and listen to my class. Often, I would finish the lesson and receive an email summary detailing my mistakes, including targeted feedback about how poorly I contextualized the topic.

Some of my evaluators even said I was talking too much in class and not letting the students think enough on their own. My first formal evaluation noted that my presence was domineering—stifling my students' voices. The feedback I received was probably justified and, ultimately, made me a more reflective educator. But it did not make it any easier to hear.

It's safe to say a few colleagues doubted me early on.

Still, my natural inclination as an AP teacher was to lead. I had to be the director, the source of knowledge, and the one who had the answers when the smartest kids asked good questions. As you will come to know in this book, I was in—and remain in—a constant struggle to live up to these ideals.

As I thought back on my experience as an AP student, I remembered feeling tremendous competition amongst my peers. I attended a small private high school of 700 students. With ten future Ivy League students in my class alone, I often felt overwhelmed. We would consistently compare grades and balk at the thought of sharing notes. I was a sophomore in a class filled with juniors. It was intimidating and, at times, unwelcoming.

Our teacher, Mr. Finch, was a fine educator, and this class had been his baby for many years. He was a legend among legends, the kind that your older brothers and sisters told you about. Mr. Finch knew his stuff, and man, could he tell a story. Sure, the teacher was the source of knowledge in class. But those stories often stuck with us, whether they were about history or not. In fact, I remember bringing in my cassette tape "Talkboy" to record some of his lectures.

One day, he stopped teaching the section on the New Deal to tell us a story about playing basketball for Joliet Junior College against the Statesville prisoners. During warm-ups, he looked down toward the other end of the bleachers to see a man with a newspaper covering his face. The man looked up from the paper, and my teacher thought he recognized him. He was just sitting there—a prisoner watching his fellow inmates as they challenged the college players, but this was no ordinary prisoner.

This particular man had committed one of the most famous mass murders in Chicago history. In July of 1966, he systematically murdered eight nurses and was on the loose for over forty-eight hours. Mr. Finch remembered watching it on the news as a seven-year-old hearing that the suspect was headed down I-55, an interstate road in Illinois that led to his hometown, Joliet. From that moment on, the murderer became his childhood boogieman.

Still questioning if the man with the newspaper was actually the boogieman of his youth, Mr. Finch intentionally dribbled a basketball off his foot, so it would end up at the other end of the gym. He had to find out. When he went to retrieve the ball, which had settled in the corner close to where the inmate was seated, the man looked up from his paper.

"Are you Richard Speck?" Mr. Finch asked timidly.

Speck slowly looked at the Joliet Junior College player and responded, "Yes, I am."

You cannot make this stuff up. Mr. Finch put on an amazing show for our class.

The kids who worked hard in Mr. Finch's class passed the exam. The others did not. Our teacher preached a message of taking the national exam only if he thought we could pass. I will never forget him telling me that I should not take it.

"Sharos, you cannot even keep up on your notes, and you have a C in the class," he told me. "If you take this test, you are going to waste your mom's seventy dollars. I have been doing this long enough to know who can pass the test and who cannot."

I took the exam anyway.

When I started teaching, I thought I was alone. I would close the door of the classroom, and it was just the students and me. As I've come to find, that could not be further from the truth, especially in Advanced Placement classes.

You see, that class I took in high school had no unity in a space where opportunity to unify existed. As many as 300,000 other students around the country were on the same journey to pass this test with their 11,000 teachers in AP US History—and that was just for one test. What an amazing opportunity to adopt the "us against the world" mentality.

In my work as a teacher, administrator, consultant, and presenter, I've had the opportunity to observe lots of different professionals in education and other fields. Honestly, I have to say that I haven't actually seen many people who deserve to be more successful than they are.

You know those folks who go on "yo-yo" diets all the time? One day, the diet is on, but the next day, the diet is off. No matter how much they eat or exercise, most people end up regressing or progressing back toward their biological mean. Similarly, many teachers have trouble wrapping their heads around that painful truth: We usually end up right around where we should.

So the questions become: What can *all of us* do to become more successful? How can we maximize our potential and even go beyond where we should be?

> # What can *all of us* do to become more successful? How can we maximize our potential and even go beyond where we should be?

The answer is staring you in the face every time you enter a classroom, an administration meeting, or an after-school parent event: You need your team. You need to find a team that is more than the sum of its parts and a team that will not accept 1.96 class averages and 18 percent pass rates. Building a team like that takes time and effort, but it is the only way to maximize your potential. Find people who complement your efforts and your experience.

Who were my teammates?

You've already heard what many of my colleagues thought of my chances of success.

Have you ever been approached by a student after class or school and just sensed that they wanted to get something off their chest? One time, a girl named Ashley hung around after her friends left my room, claiming she needed to finish a "few more test corrections." I knew something was off. She apologized to me for not "acting like herself lately."

"Is everything okay with you?" I asked.

She shared with me that her parents were going through a divorce. Ashley was the youngest child, and her older siblings had already gone off to college. It must have been tough on her, being sixteen and living through this. I never knew what to do in these situations besides just listen. This time, I felt compelled to try and give some advice—against my better judgment.

I mentioned to her that this was a tremendous opportunity to learn about relationships—we can always learn from what is around us, from both success and failure. Perhaps Ashley would get married someday, and, if so, her commitment to her future spouse will be so strong because she had learned what "not" to do by watching it first-hand at home.

Looking for a silver lining in such an awful situation was difficult, but it did get me thinking.

I was on her team. Our class was on her team. Our school was a safety net for her. This wasn't about my students fighting for grades against each other, judging each other, or competing against each other. Who was I to tell my students that they could not take the exam at the end of the year? Like my own AP experience in high school, and like my student's tough situation, we can always learn what *not* to do from a bad experience.

There were only twenty-eight of us that first year. It was a small army but a good one. Why couldn't it be all of us versus the test, all of us versus the other 300,000 test-takers, all of us versus the world?

As their teacher, I had to flip the script. On the first day of class, I held the 1200-page textbook in my hand. I told the students they must be prepared to read the entire thing and take notes on every paragraph if they wanted to do well in our class. *Slam!* I dropped the book on the floor.

I read the entire thing over the summer, and I warned the class that any student who was not prepared to do the same over the school year should drop the class immediately with no hard feelings. Everyone has to earn the right to play on the team, and the teacher was no exception. I promised to be with them every step of the way. At that moment, I dedicated myself to them by saying, "I am going to run through a wall for you this year, and I expect you to run through a wall for me."

No longer would the students compete against each other. No longer would the students and the teacher bang heads over classroom expectations. We were traveling this path together. It was "us versus the test." I used this type of rhetoric with my students daily to build a culture of collaboration. The expectation was that we held each other accountable.

> ## We were traveling this path together. It was "us versus the test."

Accountability can feel cruel. I probably made students feel uncomfortable for missing class, even if there was a valid excuse. Knowing what it took to be successful on the exam, I did not treat absences kindly. Students faced tough choices about attending field trips, visiting their counselor, or simply getting to school on a cold Monday morning.

I, too, tried to hold myself to the same standards. For the first seven years of my teaching career, I never missed a full day of school due to illness, often channeling my eighth-grade teacher-nun's advice

From: ⬛⬛⬛ ❯   Hide

To: (Andrew Sharos ❯)

dun dun dun....
July 7, 2013, 10:12 AM

SHAROS!!! I got a 5!!!! Knowing I can look you in the face this upcoming year when I happen to see you in the hall and I'm not disowned or something is such a relief. Lets us know the class average! We're feeling good about it :))))) bam! 5.

Students often sent me emails in the summer when they received their scores. When I first received this email, I felt bad for how much pressure this student must have felt during the year. On a micro level, I was excited that she received the highest score possible, a 5/5. On a macro level, when I looked deeper into what she was saying, I saw the results of the "us" culture we needed to succeed. She cared just as much about how the rest of the class performed as she did about celebrating her own score.

to "drag my bloody legs to school." Sure, I missed a couple days of school for weddings. I closed on a house and took some time for that. I vacationed over a couple of long weekends with my wife, but nothing more than my three personal days would allow.

It's funny, though, that mirror.

In late May, I announced to one of my classes that I would be absent on the upcoming Thursday and Friday. That particular Friday was exactly one week before my students would take the exam; it was crunch time and everyone was feeling the heat. My wife and I were headed for Denver to hear the Zac Brown Band concert with our friends at one of the most incredible music venues in the world, Red Rocks Amphitheater.

Immediately, a student raised her hand and asked me a bold question in front of the entire class.

"Are you going to miss any more days after that?" she peeped, full of conviction—the kind that makes you nervous to make eye contact. "You know, the test is only ten days away."

I could not believe she put me on the spot like that. My heart sunk at the look on her face, and I began to sweat, thinking about how I could respond. I was speechless, but so many thoughts were going through my mind at once. I spent the entire year dogging my students about the importance of attendance and how every day could make the difference in passing the national exam. "Us versus the test, us versus the test," played over and over in my head. Missing school and missing class certainly was a great way to let my teammates down. *I thought students loved having substitute teachers! Did other students share her concern that I was jetting off to Denver?*

I didn't tell the class what I was doing or where I was going. Obviously, that only would have made it worse. I did, however, pay $150 to change my itinerary; we left on the first flight after Friday's class.

This is what it would take to change the culture of a 1.96 class average.

I've already emphasized competition—an arrogant evaluation of data and probably an over-emphasis of my students' performance on a standardized test. I hope to make my intentions clear by talking about our scores.

Numbers will never tell the whole story of what kids learn in our classes.

> # Numbers will never tell the whole story of what kids learn in our classes.

These kids went through the fire and came out the other end—not as a number, but as a better version of themselves. From a teacher's perspective, the narrative of each school year is riddled with highs and lows and, ultimately, the unending hope that our students took something from our instruction. We all have different goals for our students. In AP, there just so happens to be a Super Bowl at the end of the season, and I desperately wanted to play the game with my team.

Many AP teachers will tell you how they aim to prepare their students for college. Since colleges give credit for these classes, teachers try to simulate collegiate expectations and experiences. One of my colleagues routinely chooses college level labs, more than even the AP curriculum demands, to showcase the higher-level coursework. Some teachers may talk about challenging students so they know what to expect in higher education. "If an AP class is rigorous, then college will be easy," they say. Other teachers want to build habits and skills that students can take with them forever. Especially in the humanities, teachers want to ensure mastery of communication, argumentation, and sourcing.

Another colleague of mine has students write their college essays during their junior year. He prepares them for life after high school by having them write under his watchful eye. I know others who commit to historiography and revisionist history, things that "academics" do over a beer on college campuses. Finally, many teachers want students to embrace learning and maybe, just maybe, learn to love the content of their course. All of these are valid goals and benchmarks we should try to live up to. We should not place too much emphasis on a standardized test, knowing it will never define who our students are.

But if a student earns a 4 or 5 on the national exam at the end of the year, couldn't one argue that the student accomplished everything listed above?

College Board data routinely shows only 10 percent of students earn a 5. On other exams, just 40 percent of the students receive a passing score. Many of these exams will absolutely crush our students. The depth and breadth of content, in addition to the skills it takes to convey mastery, provide a daunting task for a teenager. Not only is each AP student competing against his peers, but he is also competing against the select group of students who chose to take an AP class in the first place.

Regular high school classes around the country have no uniform curriculum. The goals of the school, department, and teacher may be vastly different. There is no standardized way to judge the success or failure of our students. In AP, there is.

The stakes are high in Advanced Placement. For those who teach students from underprivileged backgrounds like I do, college credit could mean the difference between attending college or not. College credit is a tremendous opportunity, one that creates a pathway to higher education and a potential career. The journey itself will prepare students for more rigorous and daunting challenges in and out of academia, but the journey is made so much sweeter with college credit at the end.

Numbers don't inspire people to be great. Inspired people simply produce great numbers.

> # Numbers don't inspire people to be great. Inspired people simply produce great numbers.

The number at the end of the year becomes a measuring stick for teachers, one that creates transparency and accountability. While this may seem like a provocative way to begin the book, we all have to take ownership of our data. We know variables exist from class to class and certainly from school to school. It does not give us a license to ignore the fact that this opportunity can change our students' lives.

Are you in it to win it? Or are you a teacher who is just satisfied by giving students a good experience in your class? If you are not chasing scores, what exactly are you chasing?

I've heard every excuse about AP test scores. They sound something like this:

- I haven't checked my scores yet; when are they published again?
- Our kids just don't have the skills to compete on this exam.
- Open enrollment is killing us!
- My AP test completely changed this year.
- I tried to drop half of these kids, but the counselors and administration wouldn't let us.
- Our students don't have the right support at home.

- Our kids cannot even read the questions, let alone produce the answers.
- The teacher before me didn't prepare them for my class.
- Administration is pushing too many kids into AP.
- The best students are taking dual credit courses.
- It is what it is.

We cannot let our students' circumstances alter our faith in them; we have to let our faith in them alter the circumstances.

If, after reading this, you're thinking, *I say some of those things,* all is well. This book is meant to hit the reset button on your mindset and give you the tools to create better results.

True ownership of data starts with a giant mirror.

Gary Vaynerchuk, a successful American entrepreneur and one of my greatest motivators, once said, "You can talk about it. Or you can do it. I suggest you do both."

To model the "us" culture we desperately needed in our class, I decided to take most of the tests and assessments with the students. Teachers typically enjoy test day because it offers a break from performing in front of the all-teenage audience.

In February of that first year, the unthinkable happened. One student beat me on a unit exam.

After each test or quiz, I would announce the highest score and who received it in front of the entire class. On this particular unit test, Justin scored a 75 out of 80, and I only scored a 72—which was good for me, as I usually scored in the high 60s. I knew it was going to be a fun day in class.

I remember announcing the score, and Justin's name, in front of the whole class. Immediately the students turned to see Justin's reaction as they clapped for his accomplishment. Almost as quickly, the students looked back at me to see mine.

When the playing field is leveled, and we start to answer the same questions as our students, we can no longer afford to be the "sage on the stage." I was just another member of the team, and an average one at that. The truth is, there were twenty-eight students in that room alone who would score higher than me on this test at the end of the year.

As a junior in high school, I looked forward to the day when I could call College Board's phone number and learn my score on that exam. It was my first AP test, and I was anxious to receive my results.

As 8:00 a.m. central time rolled around, I called the 1-800 number and dumped another $15 into thin air by using my mom's credit card to pay the "early exam results fee." As the automated voice began speaking, I nervously began to wait for the inevitable.

I knew what was coming. I got exactly what I deserved:

Two.

Thirteen years later, not much had changed. Justin scored higher than me on a test, and getting beat on exams became a regular occurrence for me. It helped cement my standing as just another team member fighting for the same thing at the end of the year. It started as an empathy-building exercise, but it finished as a bonding agent for my class and me.

We were in this together.

Chapter Summary

The culture we want starts with an "us vs. the test" mentality. We make deposits in this culture by taking the tests with the students and by preparing for exams together. It's up to us to choose how we will create a team atmosphere, but one thing is certain: Our students must believe we are not just the sage on the stage; we must be their guide on the side.

Note: College Board, *Program Summary Report*, 2017, collegeboard.org/programs/ap/data/participation/ap-2017.

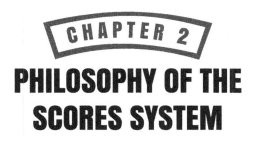

PHILOSOPHY OF THE SCORES SYSTEM

Do you remember the first year of teaching when you sat down to write out your syllabus? It's the piece of paper you spend the entire first day going over with the students. It's the one they ironically spend their entire first day collecting from you and your colleagues—and throwing away.

The first syllabus I wrote was in the fall of 2006, as I prepared to teach for the first time. If you sliced it up like a pizza, each piece represented something I learned and valued from one of my former teachers. The only thing original about it was the font I chose.

Teachers have a weird sense of ownership over their syllabuses. Most teachers adhere to the framework they create for students from day one. This is totally fair. Most students, however, see the syllabus as another factor contributing to the anxiety that defines the beginning of the school year. The daunting feeling of having to complete the assignments on the syllabus—seven different classes in the next nine months—is difficult for students to handle. We know the feeling, too, when we receive the syllabus in graduate class. Our anxiety is different, as we typically find ourselves sitting in a cohort from 6:00 to 9:00 p.m. on Thursday nights wondering how our spouse is surviving a temporary single-parent household.

But the syllabus drives a classroom system, and our classroom system drives everything.

I remember finishing a seminar with a crowd in Sacramento, California, when one of the participants approached me when it was over. "Your students are so lucky to have you as their teacher." I won't forget that but not for the reasons you would think.

I had to laugh. Closely examining the soul of who I was as an educator, I could see I lacked two of the three things that made the best teachers successful.

The best teachers know how to teach. They understand lesson design and how to assess for student understanding. They can backwards map. Great teachers are thorough planners who use time well. They can differentiate, which might be the hardest thing to do in a packed classroom. These teachers can enter Charlotte Danielson's distinguished category for a while and (gasp) stay there. That was not me. I knew how to teach, but there were four people in my department hallway alone who did it much better.

The best teachers also know their content.

Thanks to West Virginia Senator Robert Byrd and congressional support in the late 2000s, the Teaching American History Grant afforded many of my colleagues and me the chance to read and discuss books every summer and actually get paid for it. The intent was to deepen our historical knowledge and then bring it back to the classroom. As a young teacher, I had to decide between paying to attend meaningless grad school classes or getting paid to study more history. I'm no math teacher, but this was an easy calculation.

The classes were held four days a week at the University of Illinois at Chicago. Each day, a college professor from various schools in the Midwest led us in an academic discussion regarding the content we read the night before. I was the youngest one in the class by at least five years. And while I could use that as an excuse for being over-matched, I won't.

The other teachers in this grant program will forget more history than I will ever know. I liked the stories we read and enjoyed learning about revisionist history. I marveled at the way people injected their personal biases into the interpretation of the historical text. The agenda-driven commentary was nauseating. I even found myself using my first smartphone to "fact check" things people were pontificating about.

It was a show to me. At the end of the show, I did not come out with any more historical knowledge than when I started. After six hard weeks of attending the classes, I did walk away with only two incontrovertible facts:

Some teachers *know* their content, and I wasn't one of them.

Great teachers have to know their subject matter, and they have to know how to teach it. This seems simple enough. Most of us are capable of acquiring these two foundational skills.

I wanted to be a great teacher. I wanted to know how to deliver content well. I would have loved to contribute to those historical conversations with much more gusto and passion.

Even though I believed strongly in a growth mindset, I turned my attention in a different direction. Instead of working toward acquiring these two traits, I decided to develop a syllabus that fed a solid system. While a syllabus may be just a piece of paper, it can feed a larger system that determines the culture of our class. The system is how our class operates day in and day out, year in and year out. Whether we are teaching AP US History or seventh-grade science, a system determines how students will find success.

My class relies heavily on this design, henceforth referred to as "the SCORES system." SCORES not only symbolized the journey of what we chased, it perfectly personified the major pillars of our class design.

SCORES
Simplify homework
Create a quiz culture
Offer writing conferences
Review early and often
Evaluate cumulatively
Stop your agenda

My class was anchored in SCORES. Everything our students experience funneled through these beliefs, and students came to understand how the system was designed with the bigger goal in mind.

The system is broken down into separate categories. The first three beliefs described in the remainder of this chapter relate directly to logistics of classroom policy, while the second three focus more on teacher philosophy.

If you took any of these six core beliefs out of the SCORES system, I am not sure it would have worked. Which parts of *your* system could use revision, and how can you incorporate these beliefs as the anchor of your new system?

Let's start by discussing the logistical parts of the system like homework, quizzing, and grading papers. These three key concepts usually incite debate from teachers because we all have our own ideas about their role in our classes. However, if our overall goal is to inspire lower-performing students to achieve success on higher academic work, it is critical that we're open to unlearning the ideas we've held in the past.

Simplify Homework

In recent years, the role of homework in our classes has been debated. As students are pulled in different directions after school, the volume of these conversations has become louder while teachers have scrambled to redefine their philosophies.

On average, I assigned homework twice a week to most of my regular high school classes. These assignments were rarely more than a half hour of work, total. Most of the homework fell into one of three categories: 1) enrichment, 2) finishing what we started in class, and 3) creating rigor for a core class that was required for graduation.

For my students, these were not exactly the strongest rationalizations for time away from family, friends, and hobbies.

Teaching Advanced Placement classes was a whole different story. I assigned seven pages of reading and Cornell-note-taking every night. The material in US history was simply too expansive to cover in forty-eight minutes of class time. The students benefited from the reading schedule posted online and eventually worked forty minutes nightly with incredible consistency. It takes something more to be successful in these classes, and I demanded that my students complete their assigned reading.

As I thought more about the SCORES system and how homework fit in, I realized that I had to tweak some of my policies. For all my classes, I asked, "Why am I giving this assignment?" before every task was assigned. If there was no answer, I did not assign the homework. This is a fundamental question for teachers to ask.

> I asked, "Why am I giving this assignment?" before every task was assigned.

I could probably dedicate a chapter to the challenges that our students face when they exit our doors. Students act differently at school than they do at home. In many cases, the resiliency of our students is best shown in school, particularly if their lives outside of school are in total chaos. Nevertheless, I think it is fair to examine the role that homework plays in all of this and how we tailor our expectations regarding students' use of their time.

In my Advanced Placement classes, I promised my students something at the beginning of the year: "You will not be assigned anything inside or outside of school that does not have a direct impact on preparing you for the exam."

I worked with a group of teachers in Texas to help them with their AP program. One teacher, who I believed possessed the energy and the passion to be excellent, shared an interesting practice with me. Reflecting on his past four years of teaching Advanced Placement and the one "bad year" of test scores his students received, he told me that he took a month off from the curriculum to complete a special project analyzing rock climbing. The students participated in this wonderful, hands-on, project-based learning activity that ignited their passion and kept them in the arena of practical physics. He said it was one of their favorite moments of the year and that he considered doing the project again.

There was only one small problem—that project was not on the AP test. That year, his students bombed the exam.

He was not the only one.

During my first year teaching Advanced Placement, I assigned a document-based question (DBQ) project in January that I completely regret. Instead of having the students read the sources and write the essay, I created an assignment in conjunction with my colleague at another school that flipped the script. The students would create the question, find their own sources, and then answer their own question.

It forced students to research, think, write, create, and defend information. Cool idea, right?

By the time my students understood what I was asking them to do, I realized I had taken too much time away from what the AP was asking them to do. The AP created the DBQs, not the other way around. Simply put, this wasn't tested on the national exam, so why were we wasting our time?

And so the mantra, "I will not assign you anything that does not have a direct impact on preparing you for the exam," was born.

In the humanities, it's easy to find material that relates to our content. For instance, my English colleague Andrew Grieve didn't care what his students read as long as they were writing in the AP style. Their job on the AP Language and Composition exam was to analyze and write about text, no matter what the text was. He would choose text based on what I was teaching in history.

"So you guys are studying the Civil War, huh?" he would say. "I will have them read Lincoln's Gettysburg Address and the Second Inaugural Address this week."

Besides the fact that I loved my students getting more history in their English class, Andrew's flexibility and willingness to collaborate went beyond just assigning homework. He was crossing into the deeper territory of curricular content (and cross-curricular content, in our case). His class was never about his own passion for specific content or an agenda-driven curriculum.

The practicality of assigning only meaningful homework and structuring our curriculum only around what the test demands seems too easy. The reality is, we relish teachable moments and desire more for our students than a prescriptive route to learning. Whether it's an AP test or a summative assessment, keeping the target in sight—daily—is always best practice. Consider entering into a contract with your students that binds both parties to two simple precepts:

1. The teacher assigns only what is necessary.
2. The student agrees to do all the homework because it matters.

You can adopt this philosophy. You can preach how student-friendly your homework policy may be. You can even grade leniently based on effort instead of mastery and uncomfortably inflate your grades. You can do all of these things. But I regret to inform you that some of your students will still choose not to complete their homework.

We spoke earlier about building a team and how essential a partnership is between you and your students. Homework has a partner too—the ultimate wingman can be found in the next section.

Create a Quiz Culture

Many of you have found some commonalities between us as teachers at this point in the book. If we haven't bonded on anything so far, perhaps this next story will break the ice.

Let your mind wander back to a time when you were struggling as a teacher. Maybe you can think of a time when you forgot to do your lesson plans, or left your copies in the machine, or were unprepared to deliver a lesson. Perhaps your personal life outside of school overtook your priorities or you felt overwhelmed by a difficult schedule. When struggling to find time to plan good lessons, I turned to an all-too-familiar life raft that teachers in the twentieth century know very well.

Like the response to the best cartoon-turned-movie in the nineties, Ghostbusters that asked, "Who you gonna call?" I called on the teacher's edition of our textbook!

I didn't have time to create new exams and quizzes for my AP class that first year, so I copied quizzes that came with the teacher's edition of the book. It took me two minutes, and quizzing the students could consume at least ten minutes of class time. It was perfect. These fifteen-question quizzes were organized by chapter and corresponded beautifully with my reading schedule from the night before. But I should mention one important fact: They were nearly impossible to answer. The questions were filled with minutiae and forced students to read extremely carefully if they were to have a chance at success. I knew it, and the kids knew it. I hid behind the idea of creating something even harder than the exam itself, and it seemed to work. Until it didn't.

The students failed the quizzes at the beginning of the year at an alarming rate. The future valedictorian was getting 11/15 and the struggling students were scoring 5/15 or so. Grades suffered. I was more than a little concerned. Now and then, I allowed the students to use their notes to answer the quiz questions and encouraged them to complete the reading. Students were questioned on specific lines from the text and could not answer the prompts correctly, even when using their notes. I tried to place an emphasis on writing strong summaries and asking good questions in order to receive a better score. Still, by mid-October, performance on these book quizzes was poor.

Everything began to change right before December. Suddenly, students began to pass the quizzes. Those 12s became 15s. The 5s became 13s. The class average on the quizzes skyrocketed, and my students were now excited to receive unannounced quizzes.

I thought to myself, *It's working! The system was working. Everything I designed over the summer paid off.* It was the exact confidence boost I needed as a first-year teacher.

Or so I thought.

The role of formative assessment is crucial to the success of any class. At the end of the day, a student should be able to walk out of the room and remember three things they learned that day. The question for us as teachers becomes, "How do *we* know that *they* know?"

Best practice in assessment tells us to consistently encourage dialogue with students and take the "pulse" of the class frequently. One way teachers choose to do this is through a formative assessment or quiz.

As an AP teacher, I've maintained a tough and somewhat controversial stance that I do not care about my students' grades. My principal always shudders when I say that, but if every statement can be relative, mine certainly is too. The truth is, my students care about their own grades a lot more than I do.

Typically, AP students' grades will match up and correlate nicely with a predicted outcome on the final test (A=5, B=4, etc.). I've found the more emphasis teachers place on grades, bell curves, and competition for such, the more attention is deflected from the overall mission of receiving college credit and gaining college-level skills. When you look back on your experience in high school, you probably don't remember every grade from your classes but are more likely to remember passing a national exam.

Nothing influences a student's grade more than formative assessments.

Teachers can and should quiz their students whenever they want. My students can receive a quiz every day for a month, and potentially, not take a quiz for a week or two. Quizzing should be completely random. A "pop quiz" can happen at any time, any day, and any period.

I also like to vary the type of quizzes I give the students. Most of the time, the quiz is a fifteen-question, multiple-choice assessment that correlates directly to the reading from the night before. Sometimes I choose to hand out a blank page of computer paper and tell the students, "Write down everything you remember from last night's reading," which is to say, "Did you read last night, or not?"

When I grade these types of quizzes, students earn either 10/10 or 0/10—there is no in-between. Grading a quiz pass/fail scares the heck out of the grade-grubbers because they know how a zero can affect their grades. At the same time, if students generally complete the homework and read diligently, they could score 100 percent on virtually every blank page quiz.

I do not care about my students' grades. On the flip side, the net effect of quizzing like this may inflate the grade-book. However, should that matter if we are building habits (reading, note-taking, summarizing) that lead to AP exam success?

As you can probably predict, this policy will be a real alarm to students who are not used to the persistence required to complete homework virtually every night. You will also notice how students monitor your every move as you enter the class. They will watch to see if you retrieve a pack of scantrons or feverishly turn pages in their notes to commit a few more facts to memory when class begins. It's funny to observe. The atmosphere created by a quiz culture is rigorous and will increase homework completion rates.

> ## The atmosphere created by a quiz culture is rigorous and will increase homework completion rates.

Think about what this can do to affect the culture of your class.

When my students began dominating my book quizzes, I genuinely thought that my system was working. I continued to praise the hard work and draw connections between taking good notes and scoring well on quizzes the next day. High scores on quizzes became the norm for the remainder of the year, with these small assessments serving as a great opportunity to boost individual grades in class. They showed great improvement right around Christmas, and it must have been attributed to my bullish attitude about informally assessing students.

Ho, ho, ho, indeed.

When the next school year began, Jason visited me after class. He scored a 5 on the AP exam that first year and was coming back to say hello to his old teammate—me. His timing was critical to the story, as the "new" AP kids had just completed their first book quiz. He heard the juniors complaining about their poor scores, just like his class did that first year.

"Mr. Sharos, I heard the juniors did not do so well on their first quiz," he said. "Remember us? We were the same way. But I want to tell you something. Did you know that those book quizzes you gave us were available online? We searched the author's name and title of the book and found several blogs that posted the links. We found the answer keys and everything. We just studied the answers together, shared the links, and looked over the material before class in case there was a quiz."

"Well, of course I knew that," I lied, caught completely off guard. "Remember, dude, I don't care about your grades; I just wanted you guys to be ready for the exam."

I didn't even suspect that the students had found all the answer keys online.

"But don't tell this year's class," Jason pleaded. "We want them to figure it out on their own and keep working hard."

Every teacher has a story like this. They may not have tried to cover it up like I did, but after my initial anger, I found humor in it. If the students were cheating, at least they were cheating together. They were reviewing the material and preparing for the quiz by going over their notes. Even if they memorized the answers, they were getting more exposure to history. We still assigned quizzes in different formats, and those scores steadily rose too. The students were covering themselves from the "quiz failing apocalypse." I was tricking them into preparing more for my class but by accident. And it must have worked, right? When I received the AP scores in July, our class average was 3.87 that first year, and just two of our students received 2s. The rest of the students passed the exam.

I continued to quiz the same way for the rest of my teaching career.

The best and most relatable part of this "quiz any day" policy for me is the anxiety I often felt in college. Sometimes the professor would assign a book, and the entire class would have to meet for a book discussion. If I didn't read the book, I knew that I would be walking into that discussion with unhealthy anxiety, hoping I would not be called upon to speak.

We want to create a *healthy* anxiety for our students. My kids care about their grades; I don't. Let your students worry about being prepared for a quiz any day. You can worry about how to keep their secrets from reaching next year's class.

Offer Writing Conferences

I am passionate about many things, including my hatred for grading. I could probably end this section right here, and many of you would feel satisfied knowing you and I have a common bond.

Like homework, grading is another practice that is changing rapidly in our field. More and more teachers are grading based on performance standards. Those of us who took college courses in the 80s and 90s may relate this to a "pass/fail," system. Some standards-based grading is paired with project-based learning, where students have to master certain skills and benchmarks. The highlight of this holistic approach for teachers is the reduced emphasis on archaic point totals and more emphasis on learning. This pairs well in Advanced Placement courses because the goal of the course is to learn the skills and content by a certain date, not necessarily the upcoming progress report.

Hate is a strong word, but grading frustrates me. The most frustrating part, besides the obvious commitment of time, is the lack of value our students place in the feedback we work to provide. All of us have returned work with thoughtful feedback only to find our students flipping through pages to view their final grade. It's a timeless tradition that will continue if we do not make feedback more meaningful and practical.

I didn't have a lot of room in the system or my personal life for grading. I knew my students deserved feedback that would help them improve their writing on many different assessments. But I rarely graded any essays at home. I committed to using my free periods to grading the small stuff and used my time before and after school to grade the big stuff. Many of you probably share the same mentality.

Instead of grading large assessments with a red pen, however, I graded essays with the students. We scheduled them for ten-minute appointment times before and after school. Students signed up for an appointment and sat down next to me to hear their writing being read out loud. Literacy purists wouldn't call this a formal "writing conference," but it afforded me the chance to talk with my students about their work. Typing or handwriting something is a lot different than reading it aloud. I wanted my students to hear their writing like an AP reader would read it on the exam. As you can probably predict, I wasn't focused as much on assigning a grade as I was talking to the students about organization, word choice, and quality of content.

You may have already done the math in your head. This could end up taking longer than grading a stack of papers. If you teach in the most extreme of AP conditions, you lead five classes of thirty-five students. You probably cannot afford the time to have writing conferences after each assignment. Could you schedule these appointments twice a semester though? If you teach twenty to fifty AP students on a given year like I did, begin hosting writing conferences monthly, especially second semester when students are equipped to write a complete essay, answer a complex science/math problem, or complete a project. No matter what you are assessing, some things are just done better in person.

These writing conferences took some interesting twists and turns. Some students were apprehensive about the review. After all, they were not accustomed to hearing feedback on someone else's terms. Other students would arrive with half-completed essays. There were, of course, a few students who even "missed" their appointment time. I should mention that before I began meetings, each student received a zero in the gradebook for the assignment to create the urgency to meet with me. Of course, the zero would disappear as soon as the writing conference was over.

A mere five students missed a writing conference in three years.

I handled grading on a student-by-student basis, with the overall goal of assessing improvement instead of achievement. Most of the time, students were allowed to continue revising their writing until they achieved mastery. Our conversations were grounded in making a strong impression on the reader from the start. All of my students were forced to complete a solid first paragraph and thesis before I even let them start to write an argument.

The strategy made sense, knowing that AP graders only have ninety seconds to read each essay. In other words, "if you mess up early, you may lose 'em early." It's human nature to read a disorganized thesis and digest the rest of the essay with a bad taste in your mouth. If we did one thing right, we made an argument and made it early enough in the essay to make a good impression on the reader.

Similarly, I refused to accept poor penmanship. Another way to sour a reader sitting in an artificially lit room on her eightieth essay of the day is to write illegibly. I was not going to allow something like awful handwriting to prevent my students from the chance to earn college credit after working their behinds off for an entire year. Thus, I handed back essays that I couldn't personally read. I took points off if they were sloppy. Students were not allowed to type anything since they weren't going to be typing the test. Old school.

Learning more about the test became a favorite pastime of ours. Students understood exactly what turned readers on, and equally as important, what turned readers off. My students felt like they knew the test better than the graders after being exposed to so many different examples. Walking the students through samples on the website helps expose them to how the essays are graded. Projecting confidence in knowing how graders think inspires students to "out-think" the readers by masking an unfamiliar topic in a wonderfully organized first paragraph.

> **My students felt like they knew the test better than the graders after being exposed to so many different examples.**

Finally, these writing conferences will give you the opportunity to reinforce a formulaic way of thinking through test questions. You can model this thinking for your students in a more personal way when you are working one-on-one. Even though I taught in the humanities and I valued the creativity of an argument, I valued a formulaic style even more. Every single one of my students wrote their essays with the same structure.

1. Introductory statements in the first paragraph should be two sentences or less.
2. Counterclaims are always softly argued before a more boldly stated claim.
3. The thesis or claim always occupied the last sentence in the opening paragraph.
4. Each thesis gave three larger supporting details, or two strong supporting details.
5. Each body paragraph corresponded with a supporting detail from the thesis.
6. Conclusions were brief and presented one new final argument that proved the thesis.

Every document-based question and free-response question was answered this way. This was our format, and all students were required to master it before I dared to let them write in their own prose. Two foundational words provided structural relief for arguments: however and because.

Example

It's an easy and fashionable argument for Chicagoans to say the Cubs play in a better ballpark, especially because of the history at Wrigley Field. However, The White Sox stadium consistently outperforms Wrigley Field in fan satisfaction because the food is better, the ballpark is more comfortable, and attending games is much cheaper.

It's that simple. "However" and "because" are the two most powerful words to include in a complex argument. By using the word "however," a student guarantees a complex thesis that includes a counterclaim. By forcing students to use the word "because," we ensure the students offer reasons to defend their argument. Some of your AP exams will award more points to students who understand the complexity of the question and acknowledge this through a counter claim and counter argument in their writing. Consider examining the writing rubric on your test to see if this structure can benefit your students.

All told, some of these policies on writing were new school and some were old school, but the feedback was always personal. A friend of mine visited our classroom while in town for a conference and wanted to observe some of my writing conferences. She commented on how the balance of conversation may have actually been tipped more toward personal stuff than about writing. Writing conferences are a great way to get to know your students and an opportunity to talk about anything. Students will know you better and feel more comfortable around you after surviving their first writing conference.

Chapter Summary

Homework

Teachers should assign homework that directly relates to AP test preparation—either skills or content. Teachers should not assign anything additional. In addition, we have to be mindful of the content we select in class. It should match perfectly with our course outcomes and goals—no more, no less. For each assignment or for each lesson, ask yourself, "Why am I doing this?"

Quiz Culture

Teachers should include unannounced quizzes as a regular part of class to engage students in homework. Best practice is to change the format and frequency of quizzes. Pass/fail grading contributes to an emphasis on doing an acceptable amount of homework to gain an understanding of the material. Quizzing will help teachers ensure homework completion, which is our chief goal if we are assigning meaningful homework.

Writing

Assume that students learn next to nothing from handwritten feedback. Begin hosting writing conferences individually to build better formulaic writing habits, and use the time to form relationships with the kids. Students can write for fun or for research in college. In an AP class, have them write with a focus on what the AP graders demand, using a formulaic way that ensures a basic display of structure.

CLASSROOM PHILOSOPHY
OF SCORES

Now that we have discussed three logistical parts of the SCORES system that affect student habits, it's time to address some philosophical areas. Many teachers feel strongly about the amount of time they spend covering content. *How can we strike a balance between exposing students to a vast amount of material and leaving ample time for review?*

Teachers also make crucial decisions about test structure and assessment. *How can we mimic the AP test and hold students accountable for a year's worth of material?*

Finally, educators have the ability to influence students in academic and non-academic ways. As we make these decisions, *who do we prioritize—our students or ourselves?* All of these questions were significant considerations for me when I designed the SCORES system.

As a refresher, SCORES stands for:

Simplify homework

Create a quiz culture

Offer writing conferences

Review early and often

Evaluate cumulatively

Stop your agenda

Like the first three components of SCORES, the goal is to build good student habits that lead to test success. Behind every good student habit lies a good teaching philosophy.

Review Early and Often

"How much time should we spend reviewing at the end of the year?"

The answer to this question remains the same for all disciplines: as much as you can.

There is not enough emphasis on the need for more review time. The AP test reflects the curriculum from May the same as the curriculum from August. For my students, that meant the Proclamation of 1763 was just as relevant as Bill Clinton's NAFTA agreement. Covering the content will always be a challenge in AP, and it will squeeze your timeline for review.

Building a culture of strong review started in late March during our spring break. Students were required to complete a review guide of historical time periods covered so far. On the first day back from break, I collected the review guides and gave them an actual AP test. With just six weeks until the national exam, students were able to answer about 85 percent of the questions that appeared. For some students, a poor score on this first practice exam was a wakeup call to finish the year strong. For other students, it was an affirmation of the work they had accomplished to date.

For all students, giving the practice exam as early as possible is a reminder of the larger goal and a "last call" of sorts for students who aren't following the SCORES system.

As soon as we returned from spring break, we hosted after-school review sessions. Students would receive extra credit for attending the sessions, which I recorded on my iPhone. I would then download the file onto my iTunes account and post it on the classroom website. Some students were committed to other sports and clubs after school, so posting a digital version of the review session created equity. The other students listened to lectures on several units per review session. Starting this practice in early April helped students understand how quickly the exam date can arrive. It also helped revitalize forgettable content from August and September.

With three weeks left, we began reviewing intensively. We finished teaching content. We did not give a test on the last unit and began to review for the AP test. Review days were thematic and not necessarily chronological. Whether teaching science, English, or anything in between, if the history guy is telling you that you can ignore chronology then it *really* must be okay.

Order of events is important in any discipline, but not as important as relatable themes. Themes will help students organize their thoughts and combine content into larger ideas. Most written AP questions will relate to bigger ideas and demand that students corroborate their knowledge into a response. If a student is stumped by a question on the exam, he might be able to remember relatable topics within the theme and show some proficiency on the question.

We tried to make review days competitive and fun. Each day focused on a different theme and usually involved a game, simulation, or timed-test exercise. The fun ended after the bell rang, however, as I assigned review homework each night to ensure my students were doing something to prepare for the exam.

If you begin to assign review activities too close to the exam date, you are begging your students to study the night before the AP exam. As teachers, we will also have to compete with the other AP tests our students take. We do not want to encourage our students to "cram" for our test. We have all seen this failed strategy in action.

By giving a review assignment each night, the large task became smaller for my students. They completed all the assignments because (surprise) they cared about their grades. During the week before their AP test, we also began to meet at the public library in the evening. Student turnout was usually over 50 percent, with some coming directly from their spring athletic events. They received extra credit for attending any review sessions after school hours.

As you can see, review is not something to take lightly. A common mistake that some AP teachers make is using a majority of their time to cover content and none of their time to review. Your plan of attack has to be systematic and comprehensive, especially during the final two months of the school year. The goals of review should be exposing students to AP style testing, reviewing content in themes, making large tasks small, and using every moment to our advantage.

> ## Your plan of attack has to be systematic and comprehensive, especially during the final two months of the school year.

Evaluate Cumulatively

To compete for a passing score on the AP test, students must understand collegiate level content and display the skills necessary to demonstrate this knowledge. As an example, here are some of the recent questions from the writing portion of the AP US History exam:

1. Evaluate the extent of change in ideas about independence from 1763 to 1783.

2. Evaluate the extent to which the Nineteenth Amendment marked a turning point in women's history in the United States.

3. Explain the way that World War II transformed the relation-
    ship between the United States and the rest of the world.

These are loaded questions that demand a strong content back-
ground to sufficiently answer them. In recent years, questions have
been changing across many different disciplines. College Board
continues to place more emphasis on skill acquisition in recent test
designs. This is a positive change, as it helps level the playing field of
cultural competencies in standardized testing. That said, knowledge
of content is always a good building block for test success. It always
helps to know your stuff.

To prepare students for the test, teachers typically assess in a similar fashion as College Board. Some teachers try to make their tests
more demanding in order to prepare students for the difficulty of the
national exam.

How do we prepare students who simply do not have the written
or verbal skills to compete with the academic language of the exam?
Some students will have difficulty reading the questions and understanding the difference between words like "explain," "describe," or
"evaluate." This is a harsh reality of having sixteen-year-olds in a college-level course. Can we expect our students to perform well answering the questions if they don't even know how to read the questions?

As we mentioned earlier, an AP test can be "gamed," and, when
there is a deficit of written or verbal skills, AP teachers should employ
this strategy. We can make deposits by building skills and teaching
content that will give our students a better chance to pass the exam.
But when those efforts fall short, we must resort to "Plan B."

Zoe benefited from this strategy. A lower-level student in my
global studies class as a freshman, she joined APUSH her junior year.
Zoe was a wonderfully nice kid—one of my favorites—but she lacked
the basic skills that many AP students need to be successful on the
literacy portion of the exam. How can you tell when students struggle

with basic literacy skills? Take a look at their notes. The students who struggle to summarize and extract main ideas from a text set are at a true disadvantage from the others. This was Zoe. As I read her notes week after week, I noticed that she practically copied the entire book. A cursory look might suggest thorough detail and attention to the assignments. But writing *too many* notes is a greater reflection of deficiencies in reading comprehension than writing too few notes.

Do you know what concerned me most? She was trying hard. She was working every night, and I was almost out of options for how I could help her. I'm always more concerned about the students who "can't" than the students who "won't."

Luckily, we had 180 days of class to close the gap and, perhaps, fill the gap with confidence apart from literacy skills to help Zoe believe she could do it.

Knowing your AP test inside and out is a tremendous asset to you as an AP teacher. Understanding how the test is graded is another asset. Students should not be surprised when they take the exam in May because you will prepare them for every scenario possible throughout the year. Students like Zoe benefit from consistent exposure to AP-style questions. This is a free resource available on College Board's website. Retired test questions are accessible from the last several decades. There are only so many different questions and different ways to ask questions. We must expose our students to retired tests and read as many student writing samples as possible.

A student who can recognize whether someone else's essay was good or not has made the first reflective step in evaluating his own writing. The goal was to make Zoe feel confident about what she would face on the exam, almost creating the illusion that we knew more about the exam than other students and teachers around the country. If students know exactly what the AP is asking on each portion of the test, their confidence and familiarity with the exam itself may erase some deficiencies in other areas.

> # Students should not be surprised when they take the exam in May because you will prepare them for every scenario possible throughout the year.

Exposure to the actual exam questions is only part of a good assessment strategy. Fortunately, we can assess our students throughout the year more effectively than the exam does in May. We have the opportunity to make more specific choices on quizzes, unit tests, labs, projects, and larger assessments.

I experienced the greatest success by giving my students eighty-question multiple-choice tests at the end of every unit. The questions were very specific to our three to four weeks of study. However, half of the questions on unit tests were copied directly from previous tests. This way, our tests became more cumulative throughout the year, as more and more questions became eligible to appear.

Because the tests were difficult, the class average would typically hover around 55/80, or 69 percent. This translates poorly to the grade book, especially for AP students who care about their grades; AP parents also struggle to make sense of these numbers. To make up the difference, students completed test corrections to earn a half point back for each wrong answer. If students corrected the twenty-five questions in the scenario above, they could score an 84 percent, which is more amenable for the students and, in most cases, their parents.

The purpose was twofold: continue to keep old content "new" to the students and allow them to make corrections in their understanding of the material. Note that "to improve their grades" was not mentioned. This is an ancillary benefit to the process because their grades are not the first priority in the AP class.

If students do not complete test corrections, it is very possible they will continue to answer the same questions wrong all year. They will see these questions again, verbatim, which worked both ways. Some students started scoring higher on unit tests because they would have the old questions memorized at year's end. The first half of the test contained new questions from the unit, and the second half of the test contained forty review questions, which for some students were absolute "gimmes." We have to remember how concerned the students are with grades and that this style of testing creates leverage.

Throughout the year, we began to unfold different facets of the exam. During the first quarter, we focused on reading and note-taking to understand the book and its contents. Students unpacked primary and secondary sources and engaged in discussion and diligent note-taking, knowing this was our only focus of the first nine weeks. For the entire second quarter, we focused on writing. The largest part of the exam is the Document-Based Question, and we wouldn't even start writing those responses until October or November. All of this was intentional. We cannot overwhelm our students with the different demands of the test all at once. If they could just master one skill or facet of the exam per quarter, we could cross the finish line with plenty of time to review.

These signs hung from the back of our room as a
reminder of what our focus was each quarter.

By Valentine's Day, the character and culture of your class will be revealed. At this time, the students will have pushed through the first two walls (one happens around Thanksgiving, and the other happens in February). If they survive the February wall, then chances are your class will be running, not limping, to the finish line.

Around this time of year, students began to complete two-day-long exams. On the first day, they would finish the eighty-question multiple-choice exam, which mirrored the national exam. On day two, they would write the essays for the free-response questions. Now we could start to gather more comprehensive data, like the AP does, to assess content and writing skills. By March, I knew who needed more attention during the stretch run. I also knew which students didn't need my help as much anymore.

Obviously, assessment plays a critical role in any class. If you want to know if your assessment plan is working, ask the students. If you see progress on similar style questions that are scaffolded slowly throughout the year, you are on the right track. Unfortunately, you will have to wait for the best assessment of your own system: the national exam.

If students say the national exam was hard, it means your exams were not hard enough. If students were surprised by something, it means that they weren't exposed to the countless retired test examples floating around the AP community and on College Board's website. If students tell you that the national exam was easy for them, it probably was.

Zoe received a 3 on her test at the end of the year. While we did work extra hard on the content of her notes, the consistent exposure to exam questions and test gaming that we employed gave Zoe a fighting chance. Zoe's skills improved during the year, but, moreover, her confidence improved too.

Teachers must be intentional about the way they structure their larger, formative assessments. It could be the greatest asset in helping students feel comfortable with the national exam.

Sharos

THANK YOU for everything. In your class I became more certain of what I wanted be. You gave me the confidence to trust my instincts.

So many of our students struggle with confidence. If we can help them feel more confident about the exam itself, it may lead to a growth in their personal confidence too.

Stop Your Agenda

This is a difficult topic, but it's a landmine I want to help you avoid as you work to build relationships with all your classes.

When faced with the critical choice of how we spend our time, we cannot afford to inject our own bias and passion into curricular choices—period.

College Board issues comprehensive score reports for teachers' classes at the end of the exam cycle. These reports give teachers insight into how their students performed on various parts of the exam. The report even breaks down student performance on different themes and topics. Teachers can use the report to evaluate which areas need more attention or how well students understood a certain concept.

My colleague, who taught AP US History after me and won an award as Economics Teacher of the Year in the late 1990s, always saw higher student scores on political and economics questions. His students would struggle with the social history questions. It made sense. Economics was his strength. The goal in analyzing this type of data is to address deficiencies and make improvement with next year's class.

Native American history was a common theme in another class I observed. Mrs. Heldt committed to weaving the thread of native history in the United States into each unit and probably spent a disproportionate amount of time covering the topic. While I enrolled in several native history classes in college and generally was passionate about the topic, I couldn't afford to spend any more time than the curriculum mandated on a given topic. Her students rocked the native and social history questions on the exam in May while scoring poorly on political and economic history questions.

We want students to complete basic homework every night. We want them to read for understanding and not just for completion, so we quiz the kids. But we also want our students exposed to a broad base of knowledge about the class, one that is representative of the entire curriculum and not just what their teacher gets excited about. Our students' performance should not be a reflection of our own passions.

> ## Our students' performance should not be a reflection of our own passions.

Maybe this is a social studies thing, but I am sure some science teachers favor the photosynthesis process over teaching covalent bonds, and some English teachers prefer Hemingway over Hawthorne. All of us wake up in the morning more motivated to teach some lessons over others, especially if we know how it will positively impact our students. But the truth is, when we make curricular decisions, we must focus on the goals of the course first. There is no room for a personal agenda in teaching.

This certainly is a topic that needs more candid discussion. After all, teaching can be one of the most influential soapboxes in the world. It's not too fashionable to gear your instruction toward a standardized test. I can certainly believe that high-stakes testing is overrated in evaluating the academic success of a student or school. What I cannot understand are teachers who use their pulpit to inject content preference, political bias, or agenda-driven ideals into their lessons.

And to make sure we make this an equal opportunity conversation, school leaders cannot afford to do this either. The results of agenda-driven leadership always lead to a mission of one instead of a journey by many.

This applies to how we conduct ourselves outside of curricular decisions too.

What sort of posters hang in your classroom or office? Do you reveal strong opinions in class regarding current events? Do you have bumper stickers on your car? Do your social media posts reveal an agenda? If a student overheard a conversation you had in the hallway with a colleague, would he still feel comfortable with you as his teacher?

We have to ask ourselves this question: "Could one of my students feel isolated by something I am doing, saying, or posting?" If the answer is yes, consider the impact that has on the team atmosphere you're building. As educators, we should reflect on the impact of everything we do, say, or assign.

> ## As educators, we should reflect on the impact of everything we do, say, or assign.

We don't have to be drones who do nothing but take attendance and maintain order. Teachers and leaders are allowed to have thoughts, opinions, and personal lives. We just need to teach and lead above our own egos and personal agendas. The nasty byproduct of agenda-driven instruction is a student whose knowledge reflects nothing but the teacher's opinion. If working in education is truly a calling, we are called to give the students what *they* need, not what *we* need.

Chapter Summary

Review

Start reviewing as early as possible by giving students a review guide and a full AP test by the end of March. Plan on teaching content through mid-April and save at least three weeks to review. Begin to offer review sessions after school and at night after spring break. It will help students distribute their study time. Offer extra credit for everything. The extra points will help offset the difficulty of the unit tests, and the consistent review will build good habits for test preparation.

Evaluate Cumulatively

Develop a strategy for testing that focuses on one part of the exam per quarter. The tests should be difficult, but you can offer test corrections to help students regain lost points. Exams should include questions from previous exams, so students review the material more cumulatively. The more students are exposed to AP-style questions, the more comfortable they will feel in May. Do not be afraid of "gaming the test." Students will benefit from understanding exactly what test graders want to read and gain confidence in their own ability to provide it.

Stop Your Agenda

If we want to take a student-centered approach to teaching and leading, we cannot afford to inject our personal passion or bias into our jobs. Our positions in education can be very influential and should be used to promote the common good and what is best for our students. We don't determine that—our students do. This concept applies to the way we carry ourselves outside of school, especially with social media. In all we plan, deliver, and project, we must be fair to our students and put the team (our class) in front of ourselves.

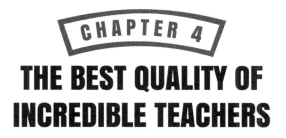

THE BEST QUALITY OF INCREDIBLE TEACHERS

My father taught for thirty-eight years and was ultimately my role model in choosing this profession. Many of us who observe our parents ask them why they chose their career.

"Every day is different," he would always say. "New students walk into your room every year. Many of your colleagues come and go. There is constant change, and it keeps things interesting."

Perhaps my father put things too simply because the students aren't the only thing that makes our jobs interesting.

My fourth period class knew that really well.

I pride myself on projecting the same mood to my class every day, regardless of what happens before I "check my baggage at the door." If you cannot control your emotions in class, how do you expect your students to do the same? Unfortunately, on this day, my emotions got the best of me when I shared some of my personal life with my students.

I couldn't figure out what happened or why it happened; maybe it was just hitting my first major wall in teaching. Everyone knows how difficult the first year can be. But getting through year seven, eight, and nine can be tough too.

All of that added up to a giant ball of frustration at the end of class one day. I shared some things with the class under the guise of being human, but in reality, I couldn't work as closely with our kids every day and continue to hide it. A minute before the bell rang, I told them that it would mean a lot to me if they did well on the AP test. I was begging them to perform well on the test because I needed it; it was the one thing I felt in complete control of at the time. I have never talked about things so personally with them before and wondered if I did the right thing. I guess there are just certain times when our humanness takes over, and the walls between the students and teacher become penetrable.

What happened next still gives me goosebumps.

Guadalupe waited until every other student left the room. I taught some of her siblings, as six of them had attended our school and created quite a legacy. She was the baby of the bunch, a quiet kid who sat in the front of the room, and someone who understood my sarcasm and even the worst of my jokes. She has remained one of my favorite students. But at this moment, I sat silently at the front of the room, my eyes filled with tears as she approached me. She looked absolutely stunned. I knew she wasn't going to ask me about her homework assignment from the night before. What I did not know, however, was that one of my favorite moments from my teaching career was about to happen.

• • •

Whenever we interview candidates for a potential teaching position, I like to ask them an impossible question: "It takes three things to be an incredible teacher. You have to know the content, know how to teach it, and you have to know your students. Which one of these three is most important to you, and why?"

Candidates usually ask me to repeat the three options—not for lack of focus but because of the difficulty of the question.

The beauty of this interview item is that everybody answers it differently, and every interviewer might look for a different response. There is no wrong answer, but there are some explanations that we favor over others. Each time I ask, I hope candidates respond with excitement over getting to know their students. If you know who your students are, it's easier to understand how they learn. If you understand how they learn, you can understand how to teach them. Content is something we can pick up on our own.

It takes three things to be a great teacher: knowing content, knowing how to teach it, and knowing our students. We've already spoken about my shortcomings in the first two areas, and I would rather spend more time proving that the third quality can compensate for many other weaknesses we may have as educators.

> ## It takes three things to be a great teacher: knowing content, knowing how to teach it, and knowing our students.

I focused on getting to know my students because that was the easiest task to master. We have to start with a love for our students and a desire to understand who they are and where they come from. We must cultivate a faith in them and them in us. This faith comes from conversations both public and private, from our own observations of how their lives unfold, and from what we perceive beyond the externals of the classroom. We have to see the simple beauty in their smiles, marvel at their ingenuity, and relish the feeling of youth we gain through their presence among us. Students are the best part of our jobs, by far.

The first principal I ever worked for frequently told our student body they were "the greatest students in the world."

Were they the *greatest* students in the world?

My favorite thing about his statement was that he actually believed it. Who could blame him? What was the alternative—to believe that we had the worst students in the world? Seeing our students through a glass that is half-full is always in style and will help establish the right mindset to grind through a school year with the same 150 faces staring at you every day.

If I were to present an entire summary of anecdotal research to you about human behavior and our profession, it would be this: *Who we are as a person matches almost identically to who we are in the classroom.*

As we know, none of us are perfect, and some of us have more imperfections than others. This concept is actually what makes teaching amazing because our students are the same way. Our job is to find common ground. Teaching cannot become a mere business transaction where the teacher provides structure and the students learn from it. Education means so much more than that.

Let's focus on structure, since we spent two chapters building the SCORES system. If we believe in our structure and our system, the equation becomes very simple. We just have to get the students to do what we want them to do. Motivation comes in all shapes and sizes. For many students, the single greatest motivating factor in them buying into the system will be *you*.

"Get the students to do what you want them to do." I wish this concept was a drinkable potion I could give you. The good news is that it's something we can do regardless of our personality. There are, in fact, concrete ways to build relationships with students and understand what makes them tick.

Rigid Flexibility

Flexibility is one thing that our students truly appreciate. Advanced Placement teachers may feel like they cannot afford to be flexible because they are the most bound to curriculum of any group in the school. In fact, many of us aren't even able to cover all of the content College Board requires of their classes. Schools in some states do not start until after Labor Day, but their kids are tested on the same day as schools that start in early August. Can they afford to be flexible with such little time to cover their material?

I mentioned earlier that I wasn't the greatest teacher, nor were my methods and planning on par with the best in our department. Ironically, this afforded me the chance to be more flexible in teaching and planning my AP class. I had a general idea of what we wanted to accomplish each unit. A prescribed reading schedule was published on my website to articulate the homework. The exam days were loosely scheduled but not totally firm. However, I still planned some of my lessons on the drive to school. I am not advocating for procrastination, disorganization, or poor planning on the part of the teacher. AP students will see through that in a heartbeat. I am advocating for flexibility.

AP students are often among the most stressed out in the entire school. They are also the most overcommitted students who rarely turn down an opportunity to play, act, compete, participate, serve, or belong. Thus, your flexibility will endear the students to you. I frequently moved our test day forward or backwards if the majority of my students presented a good reason. Many of your students are probably in the same classes together. It is likely that twenty of your thirty students may have a paper due in English, a lab due in biology, and a test in your class on the same day. How badly do you want to compete for their attention?

Ask your students when they would like to take the exam. Get a sense of their stress levels. Move the test to Monday knowing they will have to study on Sunday night, but that preparation for your exam won't compete against other classes. The point is, listen to your students. Test day does not matter to the teacher; it matters to the student.

> ## AP students are often among the most stressed out in the entire school. They are also the most overcommitted students who rarely turn down an opportunity to play, act, compete, participate, serve, or belong.

This probably reminds some of you of the Stanford d.school and their process of design thinking that starts with gaining empathy for your students. The design school in Palo Alto focuses on building empathy. Their research is based on a consumer-based platform where businesses first seek out emotions from their customers in order to contribute to a better design. Then producers can build a product based on an infinite budget that includes the wants and needs gathered through their feedback. Eventually, designers can create a product that is reasonable, practicable, and affordable for both the buyer and seller.

Can't we look at our classes the same way?

Many of you probably teach with a few colleagues who think their class is more important than yours. Maybe it is. But in the spirit of teamwork, ask that teacher about their large assignments like tests, labs, and projects. I tried this with a science AP teacher, as we shared many of the same students. My students would always talk about his class and how hard it was. I empathized with him, as our two exams regularly carried the lowest national averages.

At the beginning of the year, I asked him for a copy of his syllabus and planned around it. He was a more rigid planner than me, so I took the opportunity to be flexible. I stayed far away from scheduling my tests on top of his stressful assignments, knowing our students would be forced to choose between the two (or more) commitments on that day. We never gave a test on the same day. I also knew when he was taking my students on all-day field trips. I could schedule around everything he was doing, even if it was only by one day. The result of all this was a win-win. The students could spend more time on his labs and more time studying for my tests. They could also spread out the stress, as well as the preparation, that came with it.

The best "win" comes in the perception the students have of you. Some students are united by the rigor you create for them. But rigor reaches a breaking point when we push our students too far or display a degree of rigidity that our students cannot handle. Avoid the law of diminishing returns. Reading seven pages per night and taking Cornell notes was challenging enough for my students. The least I could do was work around their busy schedules, so they could concentrate when it mattered most. The students will see flexibility as a deposit in the culture you are trying to build with them. They may even gravitate more toward your class than the others because you showed them that you care. Notice this had very little to do with teacher personality and everything to do with the mindset behind the policy.

Designing and planning an AP class is about putting our students first. In this case, it was about showing flexibility, alleviating stress, and building trust as the teacher who cared. Now, flexibility becomes win-win-win.

Forming Relationships

Success demands that we facilitate buy-in. One pathway to achieving this goal is through a strong commitment to know your students personally. I toed this line about as much as I could as a younger male teacher, while still maintaining professional distance. My motives were always geared toward building trust with each student, all the while knowing that our connections with kids could be the difference in achieving a better outcome at the end of the year and, moreover, a better outcome for their future.

As a high school coach, I believed that every player needed to play when it mattered. Most coaches will only insert their bench players when the team is losing or winning by a large margin. This can be embarrassing for the bench players because everyone knows why they are in the game. These players don't have to play a lot when it matters, but each player on the team deserves the chance to compete at some point during the season. If it doesn't go well, the player doesn't have to play when it matters again. If it does go well, maybe the coach will trust that player in the future. The point is, the coach would never know unless the player is given the chance. Every player deserves at least one big moment.

What if we approach building relationships with our students in the same way? At some point during the course of the year, teachers should seek out every individual student when it matters. I tried to make sure I reached all students to let them know how much I cared. This initiative begins by finding common ground and shared interests. Some examples:

1. I played sports in high school and I coached. Athletes? Check.
2. My sister was an NFL cheerleader, and my wife was on the dance team in college. Cheerleaders. Check.

3. I listened to pop music and watched the same movies they did. I played a whole lot of video games growing up. Pop culture kids? Check.
4. I once recorded a song with my buddy's band and shared this story with my students. Band kids? Check.
5. I taught countless siblings of the students I currently had. Legacies? Check.

Obviously, there are other pockets and subgroups of students outside of this list, but the point remains. In these days of collective identity, I sought not to divide my students into groups but focus on each individual and how to cultivate that relationship through something we shared.

I remember teaching Amy, whom I had very little in common with. One day during class, I used a line from the movie, *Ace Ventura,* and she laughed like crazy while the other students looked at her and me like we were the crazy ones. From that point, we only spoke to each other in lines from the movie. Amy was on board.

I remember telling Jay about going to a Nickelback concert in the early 2000s. Since then, Nickelback has become one of the most ridiculed bands for their supposed lack of lyrical and melodic talents. But for Jay and me, that was our connection.

Most of us have double or triple the amount of life experience our students have that we can share. Chances are, our journey has some parallels with our students' journeys. Younger teachers can rely on their relatability while veteran teachers can rely on their experience. Both work.

Many of us still feel disconnected from our students compared to ten or fifteen years ago. They connect and communicate differently because of social media, and most of us are slower to adapt to their pace. New apps and gadgets can drive their attention away from relationships with their teacher and with one another. This is where "the moment" becomes crucial. We can still connect with students. We can still attend their games, performances, and activities after school or on weekends. We have to make relationship deposits with students in academic and non-academic ways whenever we can.

> # We have to make relationship deposits with students in academic and non-academic ways whenever we can.

But how does that help us get students to do what we want them to do?

During my final year teaching AP, I distinctly remember how long it took me to finally reach Leslie. On the first day of school, she gave me an excuse for why she did not have her summer homework. Leslie was utterly terrified and embarrassed. It was a major red flag when an AP student did not complete a few homework assignments after eleven weeks of summer.

From that moment, she went about her work quietly and never said a word in class. Leslie's grades on tests were above average, and I could see that she was internalizing our system and benefiting from the diligence to her work. She was a serious contender for a 4 or 5 on the test, but sadly, I knew all along that I had invested very little in her success. I hadn't tried hard enough to have the moment. I hadn't forged a relationship with this quiet, sweet kid.

A few months later while grading Leslie's notebook, I wrote her a short note apologizing for not knowing her better. I was so impressed with her work, and I wanted to be a bigger part of her journey. I told her I believed in her because I did. I made sure she read my note. When she did, she shook her head and smiled.

Two weeks later, I was returning tests to my students. As I approached her desk, I looked at her score and was shocked. I handed her the scantron. Leslie looked down and saw her score. It felt like that moment in the movie where the music stops and the audience is left hanging. She looked up at me with the most amazing smile. We gave each other a high five, and I turned away to avoid welling up with tears in front of the entire class. For the first time all year, she achieved the highest score in the class.

In many cases, we aren't teaching who we are; we are teaching who we aren't.

> # In many cases, we aren't teaching who we are; we are teaching who we aren't.

And while we don't always have a lot in common with our kids, we can create commonalities and value success together. We share in one another's learning and collective success. This particular student of mine taught me a lot more than I could ever teach her. Maybe this was a story of a neglectful teacher. Perhaps it's a nod to the power of a handwritten note. Ultimately, I hope it is a story about finding time to have a moment with every student, the product of which encouraged her to seriously increase her achievement in my class. She eventually scored a 5 on the exam and enrolled in a four-year university.

Regardless of whether your students are enrolled in AP, when you teach 150 total students, like I did, having the time to find a moment with every kid seems difficult. It took me thirty seconds to write her that little note, but it created a deposit that paid off for the next seven months.

There are times when having this moment is a bit easier. I remember tracking down a student named Alexis during my free period. She was in study hall, and I wanted to have a quick chat with her. I told her that I was incredibly impressed that she was the only student in the class who received a 5 in AP European History the previous year. I wanted Alexis to be a leader in my class, and I asked her if it was okay if I shared her score with the other students. The other students admired Alexis for accomplishing something that very few students could, and I wanted them pointed in the direction of excellence.

She agreed and happily accepted that role. A few years later, she went off to college to study history and education, my two majors, at Marquette, my alma mater. I'd like to think that moment in study hall encouraged her to be a leader.

These examples do get more extreme. It's a fair bet that you've been waiting for me to describe a student who does absolutely nothing. How in the world are we supposed to motivate a student like this who has found his way into our class?

I've had plenty of these students through the years. We have to trust that either the SCORES system will ignite a work ethic in them or our relationship with the student will prevail.

Edward was one of these students. He did not do any homework. He did not participate in class. He refused to engage in group work with his peers. You know the phrase, "You earn 90 percent of your salary on 10 percent of your students? He was one of those. The funny thing about students with this profile: They usually are some of our favorite kids, and Edward was no different.

We staged a "come-to-Jesus" conversation with Andrew Grieve and Edward that year. The three of us trudged through an analysis of this students' lack of homework completion and unwillingness to take simple directions in both of our classes. When he walked out the door, I asked Andrew if he thought the student would change after our conversation.

He responded, "Not a chance."

Andrew was right. Edward didn't change his work habits. He continued to play by his own rules, and his grade suffered tremendously. I told him I would shave my head if he got a 5 on the exam, thinking this would be our moment, and he would be motivated by something as crazy as that. In my head, or *on* my head in this case, I knew my hair was safe because this student wasn't preparing himself for the exam.

The bet was on.

Something happened with a few weeks to go in the school year. It was already apparent that the SCORES system was not working as Edward had an F in the class. But when we started to review for the exam, he was answering questions like "Rain Man" despite not following the system all year.

Any guesses at what Edward scored?

SCORES usually captures most students but not this one. This one needed a moment with both of his teachers and a relationship to fall back on. Andrew and I spent a lot of time getting to know Ed, and we think those deposits made a difference. Who knows? Maybe he began studying to spite us, but that did not matter. He scored a 5, and I shaved my head. Again, this bet we made was something small, but it may have been what motivated him to try.

I cannot advocate enough for making deposits with each one of your students. Teachers are called to differentiate their instruction to enable their students to learn on their own terms. I would argue this ideal also applies to building relationships. Relationships have to be differentiated, and we have to approach each student through their lens, not ours.

Find the Leaders

How do you get students to do what you want them to do? Here, again, relationships come into play. But this time, beyond the relationship you have with your students, consider your students' peer network.

I frequently ask teachers why students typically sign up for their AP classes. One answer I hear frequently: "They take my class because their friends are in it."

It's true that the social aspect of a school's highest-level courses is alive and well. Most of these students have classes with each other all day too. They share the same teachers and the same stresses that come with attempting a difficult schedule. The AP program can become a school within a school.

Justin Thomas wasn't just the first student to defeat me on a unit exam. No, Justin's role in the system, and our longevity of success, was much bigger than that. If there was one student, one leader, and one influence on our success—if there was one person who changed the game for our class, my future classes, and the culture of AP at our school—it was Justin.

It took me two weeks to figure out that Justin was smarter at seventeen years old than I was at twenty-seven. To me, one of the best indicators of intelligence is the quality of the questions that people ask. As a rookie AP teacher, he scared me to death with the quality of his questions. He once asked, "Can you explain the consequences of outlawing international slave trade on family structures in the United States?"

> **One of the best indicators of intelligence is the quality of the questions that people ask.**

I could probably tell him a little about the social and economic impact, but I hadn't ever considered the impact outlawing slavery had on southern families. Justin thought about things I didn't even research in college and I, as the supposed expert in the room, was expected to have the answers.

If Justin wasn't such a congenial young man, I might not be writing this book right now. He recognized everything I was doing wrong. He knew when I was fumbling or scrambling. I bet that Justin knew he was smarter than me too, but as the line from *Spiderman* goes, "With great power comes great responsibility." Justin could have used his gifts to ruin the culture I was trying to create. Instead, he used his influence for the common good.

We have to capitalize on the leadership potential in our classes. This subgroup of students has leaders and followers like any high school clique. When we think of leaders, we typically think about some of the best kids in the school and their positive impact on the rest of the students. If you can figure out who the leaders are, form good relationships with them, and encourage their buy-in to SCORES; others will follow.

Justin had a cultish following in our class and around the school. Everyone respected him because he was such a kind, well-rounded, and intelligent kid. Some of his best friends were athletes even though he played in the band. He never seriously dated in high school, but the girls were drawn to his personality and his willingness to share academic support. There were several boys in the class who would constantly ask him what score he earned on any assessment, desperately trying to scratch and claw their way to his pedestal. Some kids reached it, but few did so with the grace and leadership that Justin showed.

Day after day, Justin would walk through the door after school to complete test corrections and notes. Behind Justin followed his rat pack of guys, diligently committing to the same practices that made all of them successful. Eventually, the girls in this particular class caught on, too. While their self-selected seating arrangement looked more like the "boys vs. the girls" than one cohesive team striving for the same goal, the point remained: They were playing within the system. Justin led those students in the room. Everybody bought into test corrections. He set the standard that other class leaders would follow.

Justin and I shared a common interest in the stock market, in fact, that's how our relationship began. While teaching the Great Depression in February, I exposed my students to the complexity of how the market crashed in 1929. I used the example of selling my Chicago Bulls tickets online to simulate how sellers start to panic and prices go down, just like the market crash. Everyone knows that if you want a cheap ticket to the game, wait until the last minute when sellers begin to unload their inventory, opting for some profit instead of loss. Sure, I was a novice trader who peddled penny stocks in college. However, I had a little more experience with this than most students in the class. That did not stop Justin, who took an immediate interest in our conversation and started firing questions at me left and right.

"So why would people who own part of a company sell it for less than they bought it for? Who buys the stock when you want to sell it, and how do you agree to a price? What caused the panic on this specific day? Why would this affect everyone? Shouldn't it just be the people who had investments?"

It was certainly more than I bargained for when planning the lesson. We spoke more after class that day about the market. I told him stories of leaving post-it notes for my college roommate with "buy and sell" instructions. When I left our dorm to attend class, he watched my portfolio and day-traded the stocks for me, because we didn't have texting back then. Justin began trading stocks in a simulated web program and learned a new passion. When he graduated, he and I continued to email and talk over the phone, often trading stock tips and reminiscing about his class being the trendsetters of AP success.

At the time of this writing, it has been seven years since Justin was in my class. He completed his degree from Yale and is beginning his first job in New York City working for Morgan Stanley. I'm giving him unilateral control over writing the afterword of this book, the pages of which you will most certainly enjoy.

Who would have thought that the foundation for my relationship with Justin would go through Wall Street? For him, it became his career. For us, it was a shared passion. For me, it was an opportunity to gain trust with the leader in order to gain trust with his followers. It almost sounds too strategic and inhuman to think of the student/peer network that way, but I found this to be true with every class. The recipe for collective trust always went through the class leader.

Sometimes getting the students to do what you want and expect them to do has nothing to do with your relationship with them but their relationships with each other.

Justin gave me a chance and encouraged the others to do the same. The only thing he could have seen in me at the time was the competitive edge I wanted to give him and his peers. Our relationship was enough for him to buy into the system and play "minor league ball" with me even though he was a major leaguer. It's inspiring to watch our kids make their mark on the world and truly follow a passion of theirs.

Building relationships with students may come easy to many of you, but that does not mean that it *stays* easy. The child within us usually gains the love and affection of our students, but it's the "adult" in us that becomes the driving force behind navigating these fragile relationships. Every single one of us walks into the room and gains a degree of admiration from our students. Some students certainly have an interesting way of showing it.

I believe most of today's kids still love their teachers. Many of us use this assumption to deepen that love and trust through self-deprecation, humanness, and a childlike sense of humor that connects us even more. There was a lot of love in our class, and it flowed in both directions. The students didn't always show it, and neither did I. But if love is blind, it certainly is entitled to be mute, too. In our class, it was certainly tongue-tied.

Not all of my students liked me. Sometimes we may think we have the trust of a student, or we think we've finally had our moment with them. Then, like teenagers, they change. Students can act a certain way in our class and then a different way in the halls.

I've witnessed this with current and former students many times, and social media has taken this to a new level. While I truly believe in the positive impact it can have on the culture of the class, or in the more global connections students can make with one another, it can be a frightening place to observe if you are a teacher. Our students are still learning that who they are online *is* who they are in person. We can show our students examples of people who've lost jobs or were denied entry into a college because of their poor digital footprints, and they will continue to learn hard lessons about the realities of social media. But it won't stop a few of them from continuing to boldly say things online that they would never say in person. I, too, have been the brunt of foul language rants from students on Twitter. I try hard not to take it personally and, like most teachers, I would rather be loved than feared.

It takes the adult in us to recognize the kid in them. Usually, emotional and psychological changes in our students have nothing to do with us. That's okay because they are kids. Students may present a different version of themselves to us daily while we steadfastly commit to presenting the same version of ourselves.

TO: _Andrew Sharos_

THANK YOU _For kicking my ass and telling_
me you thought I would get a two
without that I wouldn't have done
as well as I did, Thanks

I received this note from a student with whom I struggled. He didn't like me very much, and I told him I thought he would probably score a 2 on the exam. He scored a 4 and wrote this to me the next year. Every relationship with students is different, and we must continue to find ways to differentiate how we motivate our students.

We all know that is not always possible, however, because life takes over for them . . . and us.

•   •   •

As Guadalupe approached me after class, the awkwardness was obvious, and I wanted it to end. I thought quickly about apologizing for my display of emotion or even asking her about how swim practice was going as the team prepared for sectionals. I stepped outside my character, and this student took notice. What would my colleagues think if they heard me spill my soul to the class? Would my students tell their parents? What would the start of tomorrow's class be like?

As luck would have it, it was she who ended the silence.

"We got you, Sharos," Guadalupe said. That's all she said, and she slowly walked out of the room.

We got you.

This is my favorite student phrase of all time. I am not even sure it is grammatically correct, but I know exactly what it means. Unlike "no problem" or "I will take care of it," this phrase means something more. For whatever regrets I had about throwing a stick of dynamite into the professional wall between the students and myself, it was worth it.

Maybe we *aren't* immune from riding the same emotional roller coaster as our students. In most cases, we have to be the adult that pulls things back to the center, giving the kids a consistent role model in their turbulent world.

Perhaps the best way to know our students is by allowing them to know us. This has little to do with our personality and everything to do with our willingness to attack the quality that makes the good teachers great. We have to be intentionally persistent about forming a relationship with each student. We have to be relentless in our pursuit of what motivates our kids and how that differs from one student to another. Parents that have more than one child could attest to this best; all kids are different, and each requires a strategic approach to finding what they need most. Think of forming student relationships like an IEP, or Individualized Education Plan, for each student. It's that personal. It's that specific. Since we make choices on how to spend our time, we must create these moments. Rather than spending extra time grading, planning, creating or organizing, spend your time building relationships with your students. The return on this investment is much greater than any knowledge of content or methods could ever be.

You have to know the content, know how to teach it, and you have to know your students. So which one of the three qualities is most central to your core as a teacher—and why?

Maybe there is a right answer.

Chapter Summary

The most important quality of good teaching is building relationships with the students. Teachers can achieve this in many ways, including finding commonalities, having a "moment" with each student, or even forming a good relationship with the leader of the class. These relationships are not driven by the personality of the teacher but the willingness to know the students.

In turn, teachers need to be fully human in order for students to buy into the team concept and see their teacher as a partner in the work ahead. Relationships help all teachers get students to do what they want them to do—a critical factor in helping students see the value in the system.

UNCONVENTIONAL AP

Those of you educators who've seen the documentary, *Most Likely to Succeed*, probably remember the thesis about the stagnation of our public schools. Designed in 1893, the teacher's job has gone through very little change compared to other professions.

In most classrooms across the country, students sit in perfect rows, complete homework and exams, and receive letter grades at the conclusion of the year. Only recently has this model begun to be challenged, building mostly on technology's momentum and the willingness to acknowledge that students learn differently in a digital age. We should not be defensive of the pace of our adaptation, as long as we have been open to seeing things differently.

As AP teachers, we've probably been the group that has been the slowest to adjust to changing educational trends but with good reason. When my district announced the desire to become the first 1:1 Google Chromebook school in the country back in 2010, I remember thinking, *Thanks, but I teach a very traditional curriculum with a test that is given in pencil and paper, so I will continue to prepare my students the same way.* There was not an urgency to use technology with AP, and it was completely justified. Granted, my students were not coloring Civil War maps, but we still worked with primary source booklets, and I lectured at least twice a week in a fairly traditional atmosphere. I planned on resisting as long as I could while still keeping the core components of SCORES and its policies in place.

My position could not have been more wrong.

The administration decided to fast-track the initiative against many teachers' recommendations, but they made the right choice. Now my students were completing digital document-based questions, doing practice tests online, and accessing the information from class via our website. My class networked with other classes around the nation through social media. We took full advantage of every resource available. Our communication was clear, and everything was organized through web 2.0 resources. I am thankful that our school made that choice and definitely believe that it made a difference for my students.

Even though we are the most bound to the curriculum as AP teachers, we are not bound to how we have to teach it.

Too many AP teachers think that their class must be taught traditionally because many AP students know how to "play" school. Sure, we would love to have the students with all the skills. The truth is, most AP students have a decent work ethic and understand that preparedness for class and completing homework is vital to their final grade, if not their test score. Why do these students have to be engaged with the bells and whistles of technology if they learn just fine without it? Because we have to value *who* we are teaching way more than *how* we are teaching.

> **we have to value who we are teaching way more than how we are teaching.**

Our students are constantly connecting in new ways with each other using phones, apps, video games, and watches. So why shouldn't we try to connect with them on those same terms?

As you read the next few sections, consider the difference between engaging students using technology or not. If your learning objectives meet the following three standards, use technology.

1. Does technology enhance my chances of engaging students?
2. Can the students achieve an outcome only possible by using technology?
3. Does technology streamline efficiency (use of time) and still achieve the same outcome?

Do not use technology just to use technology. If the activity or lesson plan does not check these three boxes, technology is not necessary and may even distract the students. Continue to evaluate the objectives of each lesson and whether or not technology enhances or inhibits your goals.

Using Technology

I started experimenting with technology long before I taught AP, but I thought many of the principles of good lesson design using technology could easily apply to AP classes too. The rubric we used was the SAMR model, which stood for substitution, augmentation, modification, and redefinition. Having students complete a worksheet on a Google document was nothing more than substitution—an important first step but not a transformative use of technology. Once teachers entered the land of modification and redefinition, their lessons were providing students with previously inconceivable learning opportunities.

An entry point to technology might be social media, where wonderful resources are shared by teachers. There are great applications for social media in our classes too. We loved checking Twitter to see what students and teachers were saying about AP United States

History through the hashtag #APUSH. Teachers and students can dissect the nightly news for media bias and arguments on key issues. Some of the same skills that our students need to compete with on the national exam can only be explored further by using technology. Not to mention, College Board's suite of resources is all available online, giving students unlimited access and the ability to work on their terms.

Teaching a subject that works with plenty of primary sources, I often printed out thick packets of sources for students to analyze and write about. There were even books we purchased, full of history sources, that looked the same to my students year after year. Try passing out one of these booklets or packets to your students. The collective groan from your kids will be so loud that even you will question how much fun the next three days in class will be. Knowing that this type of practice and skill building was still vital to developing AP readiness, we decided to move all the documents online.

My mentor-teacher began to show me how to create digital documents using Google sites, and our primary sources instantly became more interesting. We began to build online databases full of speeches, videos, song lyrics, maps, graphs, and everything else in between. Consuming primary source material was never more convenient or engaging. Even though the students wouldn't be asked to watch a video on the AP test, I used these resources to practice skill development and teach content through more engaging exposure. In some ways, digitizing primary sources met two goals at once: It gave students content *and* practice. I couldn't do that by lecturing.

Now my students were becoming more proficient with using the web to complete school work instead of logging on social media to connect with their friends. But that raised an interesting point: Was connecting with each other enough?

One of my favorite projects began with my friend who teaches language arts in Baltimore. She had just finished a mini-unit on the Civil Rights Movement and tasked her middle schoolers with writing blogs about some of the events. Jenna compiled the blogs and sent them to my class in a spreadsheet. I assigned each one of my students a blog to read and offer comments. The blogs reflected a twelve-year-old's abilities, so they were definitely a little below the reading level of my students. However, each of my students followed the directions, read their blogs, and wrote back to her students with some commentary and questions. In essence, my students acted as the "experts" in this exchange, since their understanding of the events was far more advanced.

Could you question the value of this activity in AP? I suppose. This was not on the test. But the entire exercise only took twenty minutes, and it was an opportunity for my students to connect to other kids. The greatest outcome of this activity, by far, was the opportunity for sixth-grade language arts students, who were mostly African American and living in the inner city, to interact with eleventh-grade, Latino, suburban-residing history students. What a great opportunity to build perspective. Moreover, the students in Baltimore were high-fiving each other because my students were reading and responding to their writing. A blog without an audience is just an essay. We provided the audience for her students which, in turn, provided even more motivation for Jenna's students to write. Our class was sort of like their "pen pals," but we were talking history.

Creating digital document-based questions and exposing students to web-based resources helped engage students and streamline efficiency. Writing and commenting on history blogs with students across the country was impossible to create without technology. These types of activities check the boxes listed above and provided a gateway to engagement that my AP students needed.

This is the image of the desegregation of the community. This image is talking about how black a
white people didn't like each other. The the white people they wanted their own commmunity an
they didn't want the black people in they spaces. The white people they used to grest them bad.
couldn't go to school, they couldn't sit on the bus, they couldn't eat where they wanted to.

COMMENTS

04/11/2014 10:10

Did you know that for a long time that even the law had said that segregation was ok? In a court case named
Plessy v. Ferguson the Supreme Court ruled that segregation was allowed under the constitution for over 60
years! Even the government that is supposed to protect the rights of all citizens allowed segregation.

Why do you think even governments and officials felt that this was acceptable?

In this example, my student adds context to the sixth-grad-
er's blog post about segregation, citing Plessy v. Ferguson
and the Supreme Court decision that legalized de jure segregation. While the grammar could always improve, it's the
dialogue and opportunity to engage in authentic writing that
is important.

Old-Fashioned Fun

Technology can be a tough sell to some veteran teachers, especially veteran AP teachers. I often think about some of the veterans in our department and how much change they've witnessed through the decades. I remember learning on Apple IIe computers, but they taught in an era where teachers were just thankful for a copy machine. One of my colleagues was lucky enough to retire the year before the students received their Chromebooks. That year may have been the biggest adjustment for teachers; it thrust us into a whole new world of funneling content through the device. During his final days on staff, I remember him saying, "Good luck with all this," gesturing to the stack of computers around us, as if to say, "The timing couldn't be any better for me to leave." Indeed, the pace was moving quickly, and he didn't necessarily see the advantages for students.

But if the millennial generation of teachers has one thing to learn, it's this: *The best device for students will always be the teacher.* The shiniest toy in the box isn't always the most useful. Some of the best lessons don't require any technology; they simply require us to be willing to step outside the box of traditional AP teaching and appeal to the concepts that make a good lesson great.

> **The best device for students will always be the teacher.**

If you are looking for an easy topic to research for a master's degree, try, "Do students learn better when they are having fun?" I would be happy to write the thesis for you.

"Having fun" was a perfect complement to the rigor created in preparing the students for the test. Each day in our class was different, and the students responded well to the spontaneity.

Using another great idea I learned from my mentor, students had the opportunity to dress up for a "Reform Lunch Party." During the 1830s unit, I assigned a reformer like Frederick Douglass, Elizabeth Cady Stanton, or Harriet Beecher Stowe to each student. Students dressed in character and we "met" each other through a speed dating activity like you would see in my favorite chick-flick, *Hitch*. Students would take notes on who they met and the specifics they were expected to know about their new friends. After jigsawing through the characters, we retreated to the cafeteria for some pizza.

One year, I took a risk by inviting my superintendent, Dr. Nick Polyak, to the speed dating activity and lunch afterward. Instead of just observing our students doing something cool, I figured I could assign him a reform-era character, and he could interact with our students and maybe learn a little history too. For the class activity, he became none other than Horace Mann, a well-renowned advocate of early public education. He was the superintendent of the school district, after all.

Students see more value in an activity when guests are invited into their space. Too many teachers are scared of welcoming administrators to their rooms, knowing they leave themselves exposed to judgment without context. I speak for all of our administrators when I say that we love spending time in classrooms, especially in non-evaluative situations.

Want proof?

A few weeks after the dinner party, my superintendent sent me a note that read:

> Hi Andrew,
>
> On this special day, we wish you a very Happy Birthday and a year filled with good health and happiness.
>
> Thanks for being innovative + inspirational. Our kids do AMAZING things under your leadership. Happy BIRTHDAY!
>
> With loyal Pride,
> HORACE

That was to say, "We got you." And it came from my administration or, in this case, the superintendent who played Horace Mann.

Lessons like this were void of technology, but still captivated students in more traditional ways. Return to the checkboxes whenever you plan lessons so the methods you employ can match the objectives you design. Use the right tool for the right job.

Beyond the Classroom

Eating pizza while wearing 1830s garb only scratched the surface of unconventionality. Once a week, we held class in the auditorium. As the school's most underutilized space during the day, we could simulate a college-style atmosphere by sitting in the theatre. Students could stretch out and listen to my lecture or watch video clips on the big screen with surround sound.

I remember the first time we went, one student remarked that she never actually had been inside the theatre, despite attending the school for three years. The students enjoyed getting out of the classroom as much as they liked having class outside. In some ways, it was awesome for group work because we could spread out, and the students wouldn't be distracted by their peers in other groups. We called these lessons "University Days" to encourage college for the juniors.

We even tried to have review sessions at the public library after school. This is another largely underutilized space in the community that was always happy to have thirty teenagers on a Thursday night. As crunch time hit before the exam, we invested extra time outside of the school building. On some days, Andrew Grieve and I would schedule review sessions at the same time, so we could practice common writing tactics. These ideas helped create a culture of rigor, albeit in a different space that students enjoyed.

Even today, as I evaluate teachers as an administrator, many of the best lessons I see feature an unconventional use of space beyond the classroom. Because our students learn differently today, I cannot advocate enough for changing their environment and getting them to move as much as possible.

We all know that our classes are bigger than just what is happening inside our walls. And while I argued earlier for using social media to connect to other students and teachers, those opportunities are even more local than you think. Four times a year, we hosted a college professor who would talk to our students about the historical period we were studying; for example, Dr. David Broadnax would address my class on slavery in the Antebellum era as we covered it in class. Dr. Robert Johnston would speak about the Progressive era every year. I offered my students extra credit to listen to his lecture after school. Professors offered our students a much more authoritative voice than mine and some exposure to college-level rhetoric and conversation.

The room was always packed for our University Speaker Series. In this episode, Dr. Broadnax instructs our students on slavery in the Antebellum era.

I often sent emails to local colleges in hopes of finding expert speakers and was shocked at how willing they were to speak to our kids. You can certainly do this with other subjects outside of history, too. If our classes are supposed to be college-level courses, then why not expose our students to college-level speakers? After all, our students will be their students one day. Facilitating this connection was not only worthwhile for the students, but I think the professors gained a lot of excitement from working with high school kids as well.

> ## If our classes are supposed to be college-level courses, then why not expose our students to college-level speakers?

Lessons They Will Never Forget

If someone visited our class around November, they would notice half the students dressed as Confederate rebels and the other half as Union soldiers. The Confederates would sing "Dixie" at the start of every class, while the Union side sang "Yankee Doodle Dandy." That was small potatoes compared to the "memo" that each class received around the time of Reconstruction.

Once a year, while teaching about the Jim Crow laws in the South, a colleague hand-delivered a fictitious memo on school stationery signed by the principal. In it, the principal announced a new school policy by which students of different races would no longer be able to date or show signs of affection in the school's halls. Students would face immediate suspension and eventual expulsion if caught with students of other races in the common areas. My colleague and I would act the part, pretending to be disgusted with the new school policy while reading it line by line. The goal was to enrage the students enough to feel the type of discrimination that many newly freed slaves felt after the Civil War.

One year, a student of mine really bought into the simulation. Elmer was dating a Caucasian student at the time and was infuriated as the conversation about the memo unfolded in class. He kept asking questions and wondering how the school could get away with something like this. He bought our act—hook, line, and sinker.

"This is bulls---!" he shouted as he rose from his desk. "I am going down to the principal's office right now and telling him there will be a revolt and that this policy is complete discrimination."

I didn't let Elmer visit the principal, but I did allow him to reach the door before I told him the letter was a complete hoax. He breathed a sigh of relief and returned to his desk as the other students turned to see if I would address his passionate outburst. I never did, but he reminds me of that lesson to this day when he comes back to visit my class. I appreciated his energy and willingness to stand up, literally, for what he believed in. Interestingly, Elmer is a police officer now, the very same profession charged with upholding many of those Jim Crow Laws in the South many years ago.

Some of my colleagues probably believed this drama was over the top. They would notice that our classroom was often empty—and when we were in it, there was often a lot of movement and noise. The union probably didn't love the fact that administrators were invited into my class, and I'm sure some lessons drew the ire of my department colleagues for being a waste of time.

Teachers are forced to make difficult decisions on how to use precious time. We attend meetings. We supervise other classes and common areas. We attend professional development sessions. Back in our AP class, we feel bound to content. More than any group, AP teachers feel like they should lecture, or have students take notes, perform labs, write essays, and perform all the other monotonous activities the experts prescribe for "AP success."

This could not be further from the truth.

As teachers and leaders, we have to stand up for what we believe in, especially when it comes to lesson design and the balance of using technology vs. old fashioned engagement. I've experienced this debate firsthand in working with AP teachers around the country, many of whom give me their best, "Yes, but . . . " monologue to all of my crazy ideas—only to find that what we preach, or a version thereof, works with AP students too.

I remember speaking to an audience in Anaheim where one of the participants spoke to the entire crowd as I finished.

"I saw this guy speak last year," she said of the presentation, as the eyes in the room focused on her. "And I went back to my class and tried five of the ten things he told us to do. My pass rate went up by 33 percent in the first year. I came back this year just to remind myself of the other five things."

I was so happy for her and equally happy to see that the SCORES system was applicable in a different setting. But I wasn't surprised. We devised this system based on the core beliefs of what students needed, a journey that included plenty of pushback along the way. If you doubt the system or the parts inside of it, you won't be the only one. A member of my own department accused me of taking the AP exam with the students on the national test day when he heard about how well they performed. Little did he know, if I was in the room on the test day in May, I probably wouldn't have helped them much. Remember, I was the slacker who received a 2 when I was in high school.

When the doubters come, and they will come, stand your ground knowing that your goal is to provide the students with the best chance at success. These ideas will have to be translated to your content area as you put your own unique touch on each lesson. AP students aren't that different from the others. They are still kids begging to be entertained, challenged, and inspired.

Chapter Summary

AP students need the same type of differentiation and engagement as all students. Just because our curriculum and skills are scripted, the way we teach our students can still be imaginative and innovative. This won't always involve technology, but the idea of leveraging technology to reach our students is simply best practice today. Use the technology checklist as a barometer for your design.

1. Does technology enhance my chances of engaging students?
2. Can the students achieve an outcome only possible by using technology?
3. Does technology streamline efficiency (use of time) and still achieve the same outcome?

As you make difficult decisions under the many pressures you face, continue to put your students first.

THE VILLAGE PROJECT

Do you honestly believe *all* students can pass an AP test? I do.

When I tell the stories behind *All 4s and 5s* and describe the students who accomplished something so incredible, even the most cynical of critics is silenced, or at least muffled. And while that is not my chief goal, the reason people listen to my story—our story—is because they see their students through mine. They understand the struggles that lower-functioning readers face. They understand what poverty can do to academic achievement. They understand the fear and uncertainty of open-enrollment policies.

We can always find the reasons why students won't succeed in our classes. But how much time do we spend seeking the reasons why they will succeed?

The backdrop for this chapter comes from experiencing success, which certainly can be the greatest litmus test for any of us. Once we experience success for the first time, the question becomes, *Can we sustain it?* As an idealist, I saw the challenge of teaching underprepared and underprivileged students as multifaceted—one that relied on a system, relationships, and the creation of classroom culture that was irreplaceable. But above all else, success comes down to one central question: *Can the teacher make the ultimate difference?*

> ## But above all else, success comes down to one central question: can the teacher make the ultimate difference?

A few years ago, Andrew Grieve and I embarked on a quest to prove that all students could pass an AP test. Andrew randomly chose four of his lower-level English students to join our project. He convinced two boys and two girls to meet us after school so we could explain our idea to them.

I remember wondering on the day we met who felt more confused, them or us? We shared our vision for the project. We wanted to help them earn college credit on the AP English Language exam. The students would not be actually enrolled in AP English because of scheduling conflicts, but they could learn some of the content in their regular English class. After school, they would work on building their vocabulary, tackling writing prompts, and discussing the books they were assigned. Once they were on board, I frequently pulled them out of class to review rhetorical analysis samples and walk them through the writing process of the exam.

Our goal was to recreate the test preparation outside of their class (because they weren't even enrolled in AP) and build relationships with the students to create some motivation to take the exam. Once the students passed the test at the end of the year, then we could present a strong case that *any student* could pass an AP exam, right?

By way of validating their status as "non-traditional" AP students, let me introduce the group we worked with that year.

Student #1: After scoring in the bottom 15 percent of her class on the entrance exam, she began her freshman year enrolled in our lowest-level classes. Because of social-emotional concerns at home, she was paired with our peer-mentoring program that served the neediest 100 students in the school. While she showed some growth before we began working with her, she struggled to overcome several F grades from previous report cards.

Student #2: This student possessed some AP qualities. She was definitely the most academically gifted of the group but had never been challenged like this before. She concurrently took AP Bio that same year we worked with her. The problem was—and let me know if you've heard this one before—she worked forty hours a week during the entire school year! She struggled to meet with us after school because as soon as the bell rang, she left for work. Most of the time we spent with this student happened during her regular English class.

Student #3: A prototypical high school student, he cared a lot more about things other than school work. He could tell you anything about basketball and watched highlights of the NBA before, during, and after his classes. He was not academically motivated and rarely put in any of the work we asked him to complete during the project. He also failed a few classes during his sophomore year and never attempted anything but a core-level class.

Student #4: He struggled to write. He was one of those students who wrote exactly how he spoke, which made for a sloppy, yet interesting, attempt of AP English Language and Composition. He didn't try very hard but relied on natural ability and personality to make his way through a couple of honors classes before he became a part of our group.

That was our crew. This was the group of students who would attempt to pass the AP exam without actually being enrolled in the AP class. To simulate the curriculum and give them additional tools, Andrew and I invited former students to work with our kids after school. We even convinced some graduates to return, many of whom were taking classes at local community colleges. We collected as many willing bodies as possible to work with these students. Thus, we named the pilot, "The Village Project," as it would take a number of us to prove that all students could accomplish this lofty goal. Even though we had the support of a small village, it was Andrew and I who were left hoping that our relationships with these four students would ultimately help them invest in the pilot. And yes, the profiles of these four awesome kids I described above could absolutely be your current AP students—all the more reason to build suspense on how it turned out.

Building Classroom Culture

Hopefully, I've offered tangible ways to build relationships with every student and stories of how that played out in our classroom. The final step of building a successful culture is blending all those individual relationships together, a task that may seem like child's play at first glance. If you've earned the trust of your students individually, logic would suggest they would trust you in a larger setting too.

You and I both know it doesn't always play out this way, especially with teenagers who can *chameleon-ize* themselves at the drop of a hat in different social settings. Just because we may get along with all of our students, doesn't mean they get along with one another.

Many factors determine classroom culture. We cannot rely solely on the part of the whole, and we must expand our toolbox in building a structure that impacts our students. We can be intentional about creating this culture. Many of you already do things that make your class completely unique from the one happening next door.

In an AP class, it's critical to keep our eyes on the prize. Thus, in the upper right-hand corner of my whiteboard, students can see exactly how many days remain until the AP exam. Each year, I assigned one student to oversee the countdown and erase the number as each class began. What starts in the 170s eventually hits 0, a sobering reminder that the test is coming. When addressing my class, I frequently referred to the number of days left before the exam. The countdown underscored the urgency to prepare. While this may seem like a small deposit into the fabric of our class, it was an exercise that allowed us to stay focused on the true goals of the class. Consider using a countdown to create a culture of urgency or one that constantly looks forward with a healthy angst and respect for the opportunity.

To balance the relentless countdown, we made sure to stop and celebrate achievement as it was happening during the year. After each test, quiz, or major writing assignment, we passed a "WWE" championship belt to the student with the highest score. With each belt ceremony, the old belt holder transferred the prize to the new holder as the class applauded. If there were any "ties" in the high score, the student who hadn't received the belt yet garnered the high honors. This way, more students would have the opportunity to experience the belt. On small quizzes where many students received 100 percent, I made sure the belt went to a student who might not have a chance to earn it again as a way of spreading out the recognition that my students earned. Students would sometimes forget to give back the belt before they walked out of class, which was an advertisement for our culture to the rest of the school.

> ## To balance the relentless countdown, we made sure to stop and celebrate achievement as it was happening during the year.

On these days, I felt like the Director of Sunshine and Rainbows. On some other days, I was a rap artist. Twice a year, we would engage in an exercise called "Confessions." I passed out some blank paper and instructed my students to write down all the poor decisions they had made in my class. If they skipped their reading for a few nights, copied a friend's homework, wrote gibberish in their notes that I didn't catch—I wanted it written down. I played the rap song "Confessions" by Usher, and left the room as the students wrote anonymously about their missteps. When I returned to the classroom a few minutes later, students scrunched up their papers and threw them in my direction. The students would laugh, but the last laugh belonged to me as I picked up their confessions and read them aloud.

Can you imagine the conversation around the dinner table at home that night when their parents asked, "So what did you do at school today?" "Well, in history class, I wrote about all the bad things I've done, and I threw that paper at my teacher."

Confessions made our class unique. The written responses were completely anonymous, but it was helpful for students to hear how their peers in the class were struggling too. Confessions gave us the opportunity to share a "light" moment together but also a chance to refocus on the exact things within the SCORES system that create student success. I was rarely concerned about the ways my students were cutting corners but more focused on how I could guide them back into the system.

Never be afraid to hit the reset button with your students. If plan "A" does not work, remember that there are still twenty-five other letters in the alphabet. We must be willing to revise our plan. Our students need to know this, and you have to project this confidence as their leader. We will make plenty of mistakes, too, and the more transparent we are, the quicker we can return to the prescribed plan that will make us successful.

As you can see, the focus of this chapter is not just about making every day different. AP teachers and leaders have to implement unique and memorable activities in their spaces that enhance the culture. Like many AP teachers, I hosted pizza parties late in the year to give extra practice exams. We held study sessions on Saturdays and at the library during the week. All of these things are very normal tactics to gain as much student contact time as possible.

Play to the "Edge" in your Students

I challenge you to think outside the box as you are creating the culture of success in your room. If you have to, take some risks and engage in edgy conversations with students that will motivate them.

Each year, I posted this graphic on the first day of school as a way of incentivizing my students to compete with the previous year's class. As you can see, the expected outcomes of students in our class were high, despite the trends on the chart suggesting otherwise when compared to "better" schools around us. Students love to compete, especially with their peers.

If you notice an edge in your students, play directly into that edge. Many of our students wanted to prove they could compete with the "better" schools and with the perceived "better" students. The growth in their confidence throughout the year was inspiring, and eventually we set the standard that other schools tried to reach. The focus on achievement and success will validate their culture, identity, self-confidence, and sense of belonging with the peer groups around them. Moreover, it will teach the students how to compete with anyone, regardless of where they come from or what their parents' W-2 form says.

Our kids also wanted to be a part of their teacher's "favorite" class. Consider this a motivating force when creating the expectation

> # If you notice an edge in your students, play directly into that edge.

Schools	Average ACT Score	Percentage of White/Asian Students	Average Household Income	APUSH Class Average
Our School	18.2	22%	$46,255	4.45
Our Sister High School	19.5	49%	$56,985	2.9
An "Elite" High School Twenty Miles North	26.4	88%	$111,250	3.6
An "Elite" High School Six Miles North	24.0	84%	$107,807	3.4

Demographic information gathered from *census.gov* in 2014.

of excellence in class. I wanted every class to perform better than the previous one. In that second year, when one student received a 3 and every other student scored a 4 or 5, I expected all of my students to earn a 4 or 5 in the upcoming school year. And then we did. Continue to raise the bar and apply the healthy kind of pressure on your class.

Here's my confession. Throughout the year, we had difficulty building momentum in the Village Project. Because Andrew and I were working overtime, we didn't follow up with the students every day like we should have. The students, like us, were also busy with work, sports, and social lives. They would frequently miss appointments with both of us.

We certainly hit some rough patches. In February, I assigned the students a rhetorical analysis practice essay. Student #3 didn't meet our deadline to review his work, so he submitted a plagiarized version the next day. He copied a sample from College Board's website, and we immediately noticed the "improvement" in his writing sample. When we questioned him, he admitted to forging the work and felt horrible that his teachers cared more about the outcome from this project than he did.

Think about that. One of our Village Project students cheated on an assignment . . . that was not graded . . . in a class he wasn't enrolled in.

Ultimately, we saw growth during second semester. The students were meeting with us regularly as we simulated examples of the test and worked to sharpen the skills necessary to master it. There were collective improvements in their writing, and the students were starting to show some excitement for the opportunity to take the test. In fact, the most joyful day of the project was test day, when our Village Project students walked side by side with the AP students to attempt the impossible. We were proud of them, simply because they tried.

If I learned anything from this project and the gusto that came from believing that every student could pass an AP exam, it was the tremendous support that all AP students require. We manufactured these support systems, knowing the students were not getting the daily curriculum in their classes. Obviously, Andrew and I were nervous to see how the Village Project students performed on the test, but we were hopeful nonetheless.

In July, we learned that every Village Project student earned a 2 on the exam.

College Board publishes data on what a 2 actually means. While we initially felt deflated when viewing their scores, we recognized the silver linings of the project. According to College Board, students who score a 2 on the exam have a much higher rate of college acceptance than students who score a 1. Moreover, students who score a 2 have a 13 percent higher chance of graduating college in four years or less than students who score a 1.

Student #1 ended up enrolling in AP classes her senior year and received a 3 on the test. She graduated high school in four years, which was a tremendous accomplishment given where she started. Student #2 received a 1 on her AP biology test that same year—the class she was actually *enrolled* in. We saw that as a victory. The Village Project motivated her to take two AP classes her senior year, and she earned college credit for one of them. Student #3 is now taking classes at a local community college. He improved his ACT writing score by eight points between the beginning and end of the Village Project—a huge win for him and a legitimate takeaway from our pilot. Student #4 had a moment with each one of us toward the end of the year. I remember him pausing at my door after one of our writing sessions.

"Mr. Sharos, I just want to thank you for everything," he said.

I told him not to sweat it and that we were happy to work with him throughout the year.

"No, really," he reiterated. "You didn't have to do this for me, and I really appreciate it. I won't let you down."

You see, there were not enough moments like this during the Village Project because there was no classroom. We had to simulate everything, mimic everything, manufacture everything. As a teacher, I was able to inject those moments into my class. The students loved the WWE championship belt and looked forward to the next time they could throw a piece of paper at their teacher. Students battled over bragging rights when their class scored higher on unit exams.

One former student actually took a class in college with one of the professors who spoke in our high school. These are the moments you must create in your space—the moments we just couldn't recreate in the Village Project. These are the moments that bind all those individual relationships you've developed into one cohesive unit.

The Village Project was a failure, and we owned that. But why did it fail?

Building relationships with every student is absolutely critical, but as we've discussed, it may not be enough. Our neighbors down the street asked me if I would tutor their daughter in AP Human Geography last year. She is an amazing kid and an even better babysitter for my boys, so tutoring her seemed like a great trade. Once a week, we would review notes, practice writing samples, and even speak off-topic as I tried to build a relationship. One night, I received a text from her parents, thanking me for the excitement she showed about her studies. Never before had she talked about schoolwork with such enthusiasm.

I was certain about her potential. The relationship was there. I was confident enough in her work and told her she would probably earn a 4 or 5 on the exam.

I was wrong. And while I am still proud of her tremendous effort and work ethic, I kept wondering, *What am I missing here?* And then I realized that the Village Project actually was a success.

Through failure, we were reminded of what was truly important. The project brought us back to classroom culture and its ability to drive a group of students toward a common goal. It reminded us of the moments in our class that students remember forever. It helped us realize what we do when the classroom door shuts matters. It reminded us of how lucky we are, as AP teachers and leaders, to have our own team sitting right in front of us every single day.

Words We Use

The teacher drives the syllabus. The syllabus drives the system. The system drives the culture. Beyond this, our personality, flexibility, energy, and character can create a unique atmosphere for learning that separates our class from others. But the language we verbalize with our students trumps all of these things.

The single greatest contributor to culture comes from the words we use. If a student visited you ten years from now, what are the phrases or sayings they would remember from your class?

We all use certain language intentionally and unintentionally. In our class, my students could easily repeat these phrases:

- "Fives don't grow on trees."
- "I can't teach ya nothin' if you're lookin' out the window."
- "It's all of us versus the test."
- "We cannot let someone outwork us today."
- "I promise to run through a wall for you, and you have to promise to run through a wall for me."

When students begin to speak our words back to us in class, or through letters, and—as this next example shows—on Twitter, that is powerful. We *can* successfully mold the class culture around our philosophy. *Do not underestimate the power of classroom culture and its ability to envelop the students.* Treat the class like its own Village Project and take advantage of the opportunity to bring them together.

> ## If a student visited you ten years from now, what are the phrases or sayings they would remember from your class?

Dear Mr. Sharos:
5-22-14

Thank you for everything you've done for me and our class this year. You're semi-ridiculous but I think that is a good quality to have in a teacher, it keeps us all motivated. This was definetly one of my hardest class but probably my favorite one. Now that the AP test passed, I have all this random knowledge and facts I don't know what to do with, but I guess that's a side effect of taking APUSH. Thanks for running through a wall for us, I hope we ran through our wall hard enough, too. Thanks again, Yo

Using phrases, like "running through a wall for us," proves that this student internalized the intentional use of certain phrases through the year.

Proud of myself for doing #APUSH at my cheer competition. 5's don't grow on trees!

Collapse
Reply Retweet Favorite More

Every student can pass the AP test . . . if properly supported. And yes, 5s don't grow on trees!

Chapter Summary

There is no substitute for classroom culture. While individual relationships are crucial, teachers must foster an inclusive environment for the entire class, built on fun activities, celebrations, moments of honesty, and rigor that unites. Through this culture, classes can develop their own personality—one that unites and drives the entire class toward the common goal.

CHAPTER 7

BUILDING AN AP PROGRAM

During the late fall of my final year teaching APUSH, my principal sent an email asking me to visit him after school. We all hate ambiguous invitations like that, our minds often turning to the thought, *What could I possibly have done wrong?* But as luck would have it, my principal found me before the end of the day and he shared some amazing news.

"If I tell you something, will you promise not to share the news with anyone except your wife?" he began. I could see the excitement in his face. No one reveled in the accomplishments of others quite like him, and I knew something good must be coming.

"We were just contacted by College Board, and they are recognizing us as the AP district of the year."

A few weeks later, the principal sat down with AP teachers and shared the news as word began to trickle out about the honor. It was a great experience for us, and it validated our hard work.

Strangely, there was a weird vibe in the room. The teachers were excited to hear the news, but we sort of looked at one another wondering how this happened. I had a pretty good sense of how talented my colleagues were, but I didn't know whether the type of instruction in our classes was "district of the year" worthy. The funny thing was, AP was sort of an afterthought in the grand scheme of our district. If anything, we focused on technology, especially after giving a Google Chromebook to every student in 2012.

As for AP, most departments offered an AP class or two, and each class usually included a few sections. At the time, we offered a total of thirteen different AP classes. We gave 278 exams that year, so as a percentage of our general enrollment of 1,700, we were just a small cohort of teachers and students doing the best we could.

College Board acknowledged that our data was "off the charts" good. In each of the previous three years, our enrollment in AP classes increased. When student enrollment in Advanced Placement increases, typically scores decrease or, at best, remain the same. During those three years of enrollment increases, our pass percentage remarkably went from 61 percent to 73 percent. Can you imagine giving an AP exam to almost 300 students and have nearly three-quarters of the students pass the exam? College Board knew this trend was against the norm, an exemplary accomplishment worth recognition. This data was the primary reason we were honored as the district of the year.

As a district team, we began to think about how we got there.

Working Backwards to Conscious Competence

There are four stages of consciousness that relate to the practice of self-reflection. New teachers usually begin their careers in the stage of *unconscious incompetence*: They don't know what they are doing, but they don't *know* that they don't know.

I remember a veteran teacher who walked into his classroom late during one of my first few weeks on the job. We seemed to get along well early on, so I decided it might be a good time to throw a playful jab his way.

It was a Friday in early September. Students were lined up at his classroom door when the first bell rang. I was about to begin my own class but felt compelled to hang out in the hall and supervise the thirty students who were waiting for their teacher. He finally appeared two minutes after the tardy bell. I looked at my wrist watch with a smile on my face as he was walking down the hallway.

"Hey, Jim, are you just getting here?" I joked.

He looked up from his stride, and we locked eyes. Without hesitation he responded, "Who's askin'?"

By the end of the day, the entire department knew that Jim was disgusted with my arrogant question and folks were talking behind my back. At the time, I thought my comment was harmless, but coming from a new teacher of twenty-five days to a veteran of twenty-five years, it definitely was not a good idea. My mentor pulled me aside in the parking lot that night, and, as the sun set, we were still speaking about how to approach an apology—moreover, how to carry myself moving forward.

I was unconsciously incompetent. I didn't know that I didn't know. But very quickly I moved into the next category, *conscious incompetence*.

There was still so much to learn about department politics and how to navigate relationships. Now I was aware of it. Even though I still made plenty of mistakes, I learned to keep my eyes open and my mouth shut until I could contribute something valuable.

Eventually, we figure out how to transition to *conscious competence*. With enough time, practice, and patience, we understand what we are doing, why we are doing it, and how to revise it when necessary. As a teacher, I focused on literacy skills in my content area. My students would consistently outperform students in other sections on these questions of our shared exams. I decided to focus on these skills and was intentionally conscious of the decision to spend more time reading and writing in class.

> ## with enough time, practice, and patience, we understand what we are doing, why we are doing it, and how to revise it when necessary.

The pantheon of these categories arrives when we enter "auto-pilot" mode. The feeling of unconscious competence shouldn't be confused with reading a newspaper while the students do exactly what you ask of them. Rather, unconscious competence happens when you become a darn good teacher without thinking. You just do. You don't have to think about writing four-page lesson plans or how one unit will connect to another. You can execute, and the delivery is effective.

The question becomes, *How can you get your AP program to this place?*

Despite the great things happening in our individual spaces, we did not have an AP "program" in our district. We were doing very little to recruit and identify students for advanced classes. We did not engage in any outreach efforts to attract new students or retain students. Data was an afterthought. Moreover, we had no support systems in place for teachers or students—features that should come to define every well-functioning program. Before the award, we didn't celebrate the success of passing scores on a larger scale.

The heartbeat of the program existed in the daily interactions between teachers and students. But a program is more than a heartbeat. Each AP program also needs a soul.

What we were doing was good. But we had no idea how we got there. We completely skipped the stage of conscious competence. It's similar to a hitter in baseball who naturally makes great contact with the ball. As the hitter progresses through his career, the pitchers throw harder and the off-speed pitches become tougher to hit. The hitter has to make swing adjustments but struggles because he never understood the mechanics behind what made him great in the first place.

That was us. We needed to go backwards to figure out how to move forward. Having an awareness of your program isn't always a necessity when things are going right. But when things go wrong, you must know and understand every facet of who you are.

In the end, we had great teachers who taught kids how to run through a wall. That was it.

Beyond that, it was hard to codify what defined our program. The award thrust our district into the role of figuring out how we got there. Granted, this was a fortunate position to be in. It's easy to be awarded for doing something right and then continue to do more things right. My toddler son knows this concept well in a "pay for play" concept involving vegetables and cookies. But for many schools, the opposite is usually the case. Public pressure, poor data, bad public relations, or an outside agency like the state's education department acts as the catalyst for change in struggling schools.

> ## The heartbeat of the program existed in the daily interactions between teachers and students. But a program is more than a heartbeat. Each AP program also needs a soul.

I worked with a school like this near an urban area. I drove into the parking lot and noticed the chain link fences and graffiti. It truly was a neighborhood school, as I dodged plenty of students crossing streets to get there that day. All their classrooms were in mobile units with broken down air conditioners. If Maslow had a hierarchy of needs in education, this school didn't quite meet them, but I was super interested to understand the culture behind this place.

Their pass rates on AP tests were 8 percent. Their scores could only improve, right? The first year we worked together, their pass rates increased to 15 percent, a number that was wholly disappointing to me but a painstakingly difficult first step in the process of progress. There was light at the end of the tunnel, but we started from a place that needed systematic cultural change.

My district needed this too. We needed these changes *despite* the honor we received.

Building the Program

If you could do anything you wanted, regardless of cost or past practice in your district, what would your AP program look like? If you don't have a laundry list of ideas, maybe it is time to examine how some schools are building their programs.

> **If you could do anything you wanted, regardless of cost or past practice in your district, what would your AP program look like?**

As an administrator in our district, I finally had a chance to make a more global impact on the program. During my first meeting with our entire administrative team, I wanted to make AP a priority and examine different ways we could improve the program, consciously. At first, I felt intimidated around my new colleagues who had been my bosses and written my evaluations for nearly a decade. I felt a little out of place, honestly, and knew that my administrative lens needed plenty of honing before anyone would take me seriously.

Nevertheless, I suggested that we examine the program and its facets, or lack thereof. I wanted to build momentum off our award-winning year and begin looking at program structure to backwards map how to support students taking these classes. The next year, more students were attempting AP classes than ever before, a trend we wanted to see continue.

To push some more PR after our big year, I suggested that we place a placard sign in every student's yard who received a 5 on the exam. Similar to what many schools' athletic programs do, teachers would deliver signs to students' homes in what could become a fun way to recognize excellence in our district. Can you imagine the looks on the kids' faces when their teacher arrives at their front door with a sign acknowledging their accomplishment? It was probably a bold suggestion on my part, being the new administrator and all. It would cost us time, money, and effort to coordinate, but I insisted that the juice would be worth the squeeze.

Nothing about teaching prepares you for a moment when your ideas are subject to the different lenses that administrators use. On one hand, this would be great PR and marketing for the district. It would be a visible and tangible win for our community and an awesome way to celebrate with our students. On the other hand, this could backfire. What if the signs were tagged with gang graffiti as one person around the table suggested. What if our students were embarrassed to have the signs in their yards? What if our teachers didn't buy into the idea?

The administrative audience has to empathize with this dilemma. We face these decisions daily. We are the guardians of our school's culture—the year-round employees who have chosen a lifestyle, not a job, to ensure the success of every child who enters the building. We want to make our spaces great places to learn and great places to work. Thus, we've learned to analyze all possible angles of every decision and seek to understand disagreement.

At that point, a colleague around the table voiced disagreement with my idea to begin the yard sign campaign. He was a more vocal member of the district's administrative team, but I was surprised my idea was facing exigent resistance from him.

"You know, I think this is overkill on our part," he shared. "These are the same students that get honored over and over throughout the school year. Some of them have graduated already. I just think we could allocate our time and resources in other directions instead of this same group of students."

I was stunned.

I truly was running in a different circle now. I didn't anticipate the strength of his opposition, and I didn't have the political capital or experience to navigate his disagreement. Didn't the negatives outweigh the positives of celebrating student success? If I was going to strike out during my first meeting as an administrator, should I strikeout looking or strikeout swinging?

The Identification Process

I remember scanning my class rosters and asking our registrar for a report of our top twenty students. As the only junior-level AP teacher in the department, I figured many of these kids would be enrolled in my AP class. As it turned out, only five of the top ten students and nine of the top twenty students were enrolled in my class. How could we possibly be missing some of the strongest students in the school? What classes were they taking instead? Some of the students who chose not to take my class were enrolled in other AP courses. But this was AP US History, the AP's longest running class and the hallmark course of Advanced Placement. Our students didn't know that, but I did, and I couldn't imagine top students foregoing a class that had great potential in launching their postsecondary careers.

Our problem was a microcosm of the larger issue: We had no systematic way to identify and encourage our students to challenge themselves. Members of each department were asked for recommendations for next year's courses. Counselors met with students briefly to discuss classes for the upcoming year. Many of the elective departments recruited hard and showcased their offerings. These efforts contributed to some education about options. But we were missing a key component that would come to revolutionize this process for our district.

What are the qualities that define the best AP students in your class?

If you were to average the ACT scores of all of my students who took my AP class over the years, the mean score was a 22. Many of the public schools around ours maintained a *schoolwide* average of 24, 25, or 26 among larger student populations that ranged from 1500 to 3500. This means, the average student at a neighboring school probably scored higher than most of my AP students on the defining standardized test in high school. It's hard to say that raw intelligence or test-taking mastery are qualities that define the most abled AP students. We had the best APUSH scores in the state of Illinois, and my students weren't exactly scoring 27s on the ACT.

Again, I could reference socioeconomic challenges, cultural roadblocks, lack of parent support, and everything else in between. But there's no sense in that. Instead of placing a focus on what your students don't have, place a focus on what they do have.

During my writing conferences with Lisa, we often discussed her story and the path she took to my AP class. During her first year, she was tagged as "Academy" level, a track we offered students who scored in the lowest 20 percent of our incoming class on their entrance exam. The size of these classes capped at seventeen, and the pace of content coverage was much slower. The Academy classes focused on skill building in order to help students close the gap, with the eventual goal of enrolling in more challenging courses as upperclassmen. Lisa certainly took this to heart and then some. She decided to take Advanced Placement European History, a class akin to the difficulty of ours. For Lisa, the challenge would be even greater coming from Academy into AP— and doing so as a sophomore. Lisa struggled through European History, earning a C in the class and a 1 on the AP exam.

> # Instead of placing a focus on what your students don't have, place a focus on what they do have.

College Board studies show that students have a better chance of completing a college degree if they *don't take an AP class* than if they take an AP class and receive a 1. This is a deflating statistic, especially for a student as positive as Lisa.

We often talked about her score and how she felt confident that she could do better. Gradually throughout the year, her notes improved, her test scores rose to the class average, and her writing reflected a level of progress that was encouraging. Lisa bought into SCORES, but the system didn't carry this student through—her own determination did. Lisa really wanted to pass the test at the end of the year. She wanted to prove to her mother, and her former teacher, that the previous year was a fluke and that she was a student capable of so much more. She wanted to prove to me that our year would be different. I often reminded Lisa of how happy I was that she received a 1 the year before because it influenced (in a positive way) the quality of her work in my class. The experience would make her story even better.

My students desperately wanted to prove that they belonged and wanted to prove it to those around them. They possessed the work ethic and the determination to believe in themselves and in each other. They were gritty, the type of grit you want in the people fighting next to you in a battle.

Lisa's grit was her defining quality during her junior year. The Cs she received sophomore year became Bs the year after. And because scores do matter, I'll mention that Lisa fought her way to a 4 on the AP exam in what became my favorite underdog story.

So how do you measure grit and toughness?

We survey our students at the beginning of every year to examine different qualities that may lead to AP class success. Here are a few examples of the kinds of questions we ask:

- What do you do when you are faced with a challenge?
- How do you respond to someone when they tell you that you cannot do something?
- Do you believe your current courses challenge you?
- Which class has been your favorite so far and why?
- Who are three adults in the building that you trust?
- Are you thinking about college?
- What do you want to do when you grow up?

The more questions we ask, the more we learn about a student's potential and the qualities they possess that may lead toward more challenging coursework. We compile this survey data in a spread-sheet, which provides anecdotal data on who our students are. Our teachers also answer questions about the students and whether or not they have AP potential. Most schools have a process for recommending students. But instead of asking about grades or test scores, we ask teachers to recommend students based on potential—a strong nod to the power of grit, determination, and the work ethic it takes to be successful.

The AP Team

During the process of identifying students with AP potential, we form an "AP" team of fifteen adults from different curricular areas to begin the identification process. There are some AP teachers in the room, but we value the opinions of our special education and physical education teachers just as much, as their interactions with students often reveal the qualities we look for. The selection of the team is extraordinarily important, as this team has the ability to change the trajectory of so many students through AP. Thus, the team must include "pro-student" adults—those who believe in our kids and their potential. The team must also include folks who have the respect of the entire faculty. We don't want the process to seem like an administrative initiative, and we need trustworthy team members who deliver honest messages to the rest of the staff. If you can find teachers who put their students first, show willingness to contribute their time, and command tremendous respect from their colleagues, you've found yourself some great teammates.

Each student with a 2.5 GPA or higher is individually discussed using all of our data. We also look at standardized test performance and College Board's AP potential reports. We try and customize a recommendation for each student with AP potential. It makes more sense to recommend specific AP courses to students who have an interest in the curricular area. In fact, one of the schools I've worked with in Pearland, Texas, does this best, as they offer eight different career paths and prescribe the exact AP course pathway to get students there.

As of last year, we ranked in the top 1 percent of schools in the nation in achieving racial and socioeconomic equity in our AP program. Twenty percent of our school is made up of middle-to-low income male Latino students, and nineteen percent of our AP rosters are filled with this same subgroup. This process doesn't involve intersectionality, nor do we speak of our students and their paths in relation to their racial subgroups, but we see the byproduct of this work as the equality of opportunity we create for all students. We value each student as an individual.

The team must recommend a specific AP course, as opposed to *any* AP course. As you review the process for identification in your school, match students with courses using the following criteria:

1. What is the student interested in?
2. What class is he or she most prepared for?
3. Which exam might give him or her the best chance to succeed?

Questions two and three are actually different. Students should show some proficiency in "feeder" classes before they plunge into Advanced Placement. But not all Advanced Placement courses are created equal. Some classes like AP Spanish language, AP Seminar, and AP Psychology have higher pass rates and are generally entry-level AP courses. We should recommend more of these classes to first-time AP students than, say, APUSH, AP Physics, or AP Calculus. At our school, we encourage native speakers to take the Spanish language class their junior year. Most of our students pass the exam and approach their senior year AP classes with way more confidence having passed an AP test already. We want the students to be successful as early as possible to maximize the opportunities they may have as upperclassmen.

Of course, this process isn't all about Advanced Placement. We have plenty of students who own a 2.5 GPA that may not be ready for AP. Through consultation with the teachers in the room and a hard look at the data, many of our students are recommended to move from lower-level classes to core classes or from core classes to honors classes. The entire process is about "raising the bar" and seeing the potential in students they may not see in themselves. This stage of identification is crucial to the success of all your students.

Equally important is the role of the administration.

If your school is interested in making AP a priority, your program must have a guardian. This person must take ultimate ownership of the process. Our guardian was our principal, Dr. Tatiana Bonuma, who set the agenda for every meeting, led the conversation about every student, and followed up on the outreach and support systems. She was invested in each student we spoke about and trusted the adults in the room. Tatiana allowed all of us to have input. She kept the entire team focused so that every discussion was treated with fidelity. Simply put, she was the leader.

If you intend on having a well-functioning AP program, the principal has to take ownership of this process and work alongside the staff, having both the vision for each student's path and the willingness to do the work. Another administrator in the building could also serve in this role, but when the instructional leader of the building is invested in the process, it sends a strong message that the initiative matters. Our staff will tell you that our principal's involvement in the process is the biggest reason why the AP team is successful. The job of the principal usually fits somewhere between restaurant manager and cheerleader, but in this case, showing the willingness to roll up her sleeves and have meaningful conversations about students makes all the difference.

We must be real with one another too. Some students are not ready for AP yet, and as building leaders, we must support this. The teachers in the room know the students better than the administrators do.

We have to have faith that the AP program can serve as a catalyst for improving the overall culture at the school. We've experienced the results. In the last four years, our school has doubled the number of students taking AP classes. On the flip side, we've decreased the number of students taking remedial classes. It makes sense to prioritize your school's Advanced Placement program if you are a building administrator or instructional leader who is constantly looking at the global view of outcomes at your school. There is a trickle-down effect from the top, as more students will continue to view the AP program as a destination and not just a dream. In an ideal world, a student should be able to tell you exactly what he or she needs to do to become an AP student. Your program should be *that* transparent and articulated. If this process includes the examination of every student's individual path toward success, chances are the school's trajectory will continue to point upwards.

> **In an ideal world, a student should be able to tell you exactly what he or she needs to do to become an AP student. Your program should be that transparent and articulated.**

What if Lisa's confidence was shattered by the C she received in her first AP class? What if she decided not to take another AP class after she scored a 1 on the AP Euro test? What if she returned to the lower-level classes where she started her high school career? We speak about students like Lisa frequently in our meetings, as she maintains good grades and possesses many qualities that we are looking for in AP students. We cannot afford to give up on students like her after one year because there are plenty of other "Lisas" in our program— and in yours.

Outreach and Support

Once the team identifies students for Advanced Placement courses, recruitment and retention of students becomes paramount. This process includes collective and individual efforts of the AP team and faculty to ensure that our conversations about our students result in tangible results during course selection.

We start by inviting prospective AP students to a meeting about the benefits of advanced classes. Our faculty runs the event, and we acknowledge student attendance by handing out cookies. We survey the students about their AP intentions to determine which students are "all-in" and which students will require more convincing. Next, parents receive an invitation to a bilingual presentation about the AP program and its benefits. Former AP students address the future AP families and highlight the opportunities they've experienced in our program. This helps build momentum. If we achieve a combination of the parents and the school educating the students on the benefits of AP, we've formed the most formidable partnership capable of reaching a student, and we will increase our chances of future parental support in the process.

If a student is still not interested in AP, we assign a "trusted adult" in the building to speak to the student individually. We choose the adult based on the feedback we receive in the student surveys. Each trusted adult participates in a training session before these conversations, as we want the adults to gain familiarity with each student's situation and our outreach process.

Through all of this, some of our students won't choose to take an AP class, which is completely acceptable to us, especially if we learn about new obstacles and challenges in their lives during the process. Rest assured, once students find themselves on our outreach list, we will throw our best pitches in hopes they'll see the same potential in themselves as we see in them.

Once students are enrolled in AP classes, especially the students who didn't fit the "profile" of an AP student (whatever that means), our job is to support them. In our program, our teachers were tasked with supporting the influx of new students. These support systems grew organically based on student surveys and innovative ideas from our staff.

When we asked our students for feedback about barriers to AP enrollment, the two most consistent responses were 1) lack of encouragement from adults and 2) needing a sense of belonging. Thus if our students are trained to have a growth mindset (intelligence is not fixed), our staff can design programs to build a culture of belonging.

There are some support systems that address stress, like our morning yoga program for students who need physical activity to help with AP anxiety. However, the bulk of our support systems facilitate more time for teachers and students to spend together. In the two weeks before school begins, we schedule "office hours" for AP teachers. Any AP student can visit his or her teacher to ask questions about the course or the summer homework. This allows students to gain a familiarity with their teachers before the school year begins. New AP students eat breakfast with their AP teachers once a month during the school year and are given time to ask additional questions about classwork. We offer the same program during lunch periods. Finally, we host barbecues after school and before home football games for AP students to help build the "us" culture. Whether it is academic or social time, supporting an AP community is a mandate for program leaders. AP teachers are not the only ones who fight for more time. We've consistently heard that our students want more time with their teachers. District leaders must facilitate this exchange, investing either financially or through creative scheduling to make it happen.

We try to replicate this process with the schools we work with around the country, fully knowing that each school faces unique challenges and has different areas of potential growth.

We spent two days working with a staff near Detroit and encountered a staff member who gave us a hard time. Ironically, he was a department chair and taught the largest percentage of AP students in the school. Throughout the sessions, he questioned our process, outwardly highlighting the differences between our school and theirs. While no two schools are identical, the core beliefs and values behind all of our processes and support systems are the same—we can always do better. Our goal is to instill this belief in every staff we work with. The best chance at drowning out negativity at our schools is to attack it with an onslaught of positive, pro-student, hopeful energy that becomes contagious. We continued to show him, not tell him. Our team countered every one of his negative punches and observed his colleagues around him beginning to roll their eyes at his questions.

By the end of the second day, we finished our session by showing a video we made about our program. He saw the swelling of positive energy from the staff, students, parents, and community. I remember the look on his face before he raised his hand one final time and prepared another comment for us in front of his peers.

"So, basically, I think this all boils down to one thing," he mused aloud, coming to his final conclusion. "You guys have a great culture in your program. It all comes back to the culture you've worked to create in your school."

Exactly.

The hallmark of our support systems focuses on just that as we invest heavily in a one-week summer readiness camp that focuses on building program culture. Many schools choose skill development or booster courses as their summer undertaking. We are not convinced that students can make substantial gains in the limited amount of time we have them in the summer. Moreover, culture should come first as the foundation of the AP program, which will allow for a more palatable delivery of skills during the school year.

Nearly one hundred first-time AP students participate in our program, led by five teachers and a counselor. We spend a full day on a college campus to encourage students toward the loftier goals of post-secondary education. The group also visits a museum in Chicago and competes in a scavenger hunt in smaller groups. In between the trips, students work on growth mindset and collaborative activities meant to encourage relationships and build a network within our community. The teachers remain by their sides throughout the week, ensuring that students are inspired and always well-fed. We try to generate more momentum by tweeting out pictures from the week and buying T-shirts for the participants. This way, the energy continues throughout the school year and students are reminded of the things they learned in the summer.

After tracking data for several years, we found that new Advanced Placement students who enrolled in the summer program scored 11 percent higher than those who did not—a piece of data we continue to leverage with our staff and students. Sometimes anecdotal data proves worthy in evaluating a program's success, but hard numbers don't lie. Academic gains can be difficult to attain in the summer. But the AP Readiness Camp helps students feel a part of something special and creates cultural deposits that we believe make a significant difference in our achievement rates.

Our new friend in Detroit probably made it sound too easy. But building these types of support systems involves assembling a like-minded team and a commitment to marketing its purpose to the most skeptical folks in the school. This has been a four-year project motivated mostly by a "So now what?" attitude following the

AP students visit Loyola University in downtown
Chicago during our AP Summer Readiness Camp.
Of course, the T-shirts are always a hit.

recognition we received from College Board. As we discussed earlier, we became an award-winning school before we consciously created an award-winning culture.

Your school has the opportunity to do this in the proper order. Each of us has the power to make positive cultural deposits in our space, and our efforts can certainly make a difference on a global scale. Remember, a teacher can increase their test scores simply by creating a good system. But a program will never rise to the next level without administrative support, a process-driven approach to identification and outreach, and the support systems that assist all AP students and teachers. We continue to build on that culture today, knowing that we, too, can always do better.

> ## Each of us has the power to make positive cultural deposits in our space, and our efforts can certainly make a difference on a global scale.

Building Community

What is your AP program doing to ensure support for every student and enable a culture of success to grow?

While my colleague continued to belabor his disagreement about my yard sign idea, I thought to myself, *So what if we honor the same students over and over again?* I didn't see any harm in creating additional celebration for our student's accomplishments. Thankfully, my superintendent saw it the same way, and the sign campaign signaled a brand-new day for AP in our district. No longer would we accept excellence happening in isolation. Now, our mission was to create a program capable of bleeding into the fabric of our entire school, one that would encourage more students to reach their potential, while promising consistent support along the way.

The signs were never about recognizing the students. The signs helped us recognize the *parents* who were our critical partners in supporting our kids. The signs also helped us generate goodwill with our community. Imagine being a homeowner with a $6,000 property tax bill going mostly toward the local high school. Wouldn't you feel better about your investment after seeing these signs around the community?

I remember meeting a student's grandfather a few years ago when we knocked on the door to deliver a sign. Once he figured out why we were there, he called his wife downstairs to meet us. They stood at the

Spanish teacher Rich Drobny pictured with one of our juniors, Liliana Gaona. Liliana speaks to all our incoming AP students about the expectations, experiences, and energy it takes to enroll in AP. She will attend a four-year university next year to study Spanish.

Our signs are a source of great pride for our students, parents, and community.

front door, arm in arm, shedding tears of joy for the accomplishment of their granddaughter.

At first, we were stunned to see how much it meant to this family. Later, I would find out how the elderly couple took custody of the student after her dad was jailed and her mom passed away. They sent us a handwritten thank you note explaining all of this, a validation that any form of recognition can be impactful. Stories like this remind us that even the simplest of gestures creates moments in people's lives that we cannot even comprehend. For this family, the sign was not just a celebration, but it was also a symbol of their commitment to their granddaughter.

These signs also gave us the opportunity to connect teachers and students after the school year in a celebration that some students claimed to be more fun than scoring a 5.

Every time we place signs throughout the community, we return with great stories. My favorite story happened when one of our teachers arrived at a house, only to find the student was at work. His dad was home and shared that the student was in Park Ridge, a town nearly twenty minutes away, working at SportsMart. Instead of leaving the sign in the yard, the teacher drove to the store. He waited in line with the other customers, and he awarded the student with his sign. All the customers in the store cheered his accomplishment.

When we began delivering signs, administrators were the ones going door to door. Now, the teachers won't let us do it, often using their summer break to deliver the signs and, more importantly, create the memories.

It started with a sign, but it continued with the support of many different stakeholders—a true "sign" that the best programs cannot thrive on great teaching alone but require leadership that is equal parts visionary and reflective.

AP Program Tools

Identification Tools

1. Use PSAT data or the state's equivalent standardized test data.
2. Use GPA as an indicator of work ethic, starting with 2.5 and above—or 2.75 and above for a more conservative approach.
3. Administer a student survey to identify growth mindset, determination, and which adults the students trust.
4. Have every adult in the building answer similar questions about all of the students. The more adult advocates we can find, the more AP students we can find.
5. Develop a pathway in each department to reach AP classes and use teacher recommendations.

Outreach Tools

1. Personally invite each identified student to a large presentation about AP classes.
2. Host a parent night and encourage former AP students to speak to prospective AP students and parents.
3. Assign a trusted adult to personally speak to each student and recommend a specific class or two.
4. Take pictures of AP teachers and post them around the school in the "We Want You for AP" parody of the old military poster.
5. Create a video where teachers and students can market the program digitally.

Support Tools

1. Host a summer readiness program that focuses on building culture for all first-time AP students.
2. Have AP teachers articulate their tests to one another.

3. Develop an intensive, but quick, summer program that focuses on common skills like writing across content areas.
4. Post a yard sign in each student's lawn to recognize the courage behind AP enrollment.
5. Host breakfast and lunch events for AP students and teachers during the school year.
6. Survey students frequently about what they want and need from the program.

Sign delivery usually happens the week before school starts. It gives returning students excitement to begin the school year and gives future AP students a goal to work toward.

Chapter Summary

If teachers are willing to take risks and make changes to their system, administrators and those folks in support roles must be willing to do the same. Supporting an AP program begins by building an AP team that is representative of different stakeholders who are concerned with students' success.

Next, the team must work strategically to gather data on students and make targeted outreach efforts toward potential AP students. We are not always looking for more students; we are looking for the "right" students—the product of which might be more students. Either way, the goal is to develop an outreach plan to ensure students enroll in challenging AP classes. Once they enroll, the team can begin to build support systems for those students. By listening to our kids and their teachers, we can design a program that supports all our students. This entire process should be driven by the principal, who must listen but also lead. Everyone in the building must understand the who, what, where, when, and why behind the initiative.

Finally, a great AP program invests in celebrating success. The parents and the community will help support the program as we acknowledge the amazing accomplishments of the students.

LIFE IN THE "WOULDS"

I often wonder how teachers will use this book. Maybe it will be something assigned to you as a part of the district's professional development plan. If this is the case, I would be thrilled if you made it this far! Maybe you stumbled upon it as a recommendation from a friend. Hopefully you've enjoyed a feel-good story and gained inspiration from the challenges we overcame.

But if you are reading this book as an Advanced Placement teacher or administrator who wants to improve your scores and your program, I can tell you one thing about the journey: It will not be easy. You know this already because teaching is not easy. Being a successful teacher is even harder, especially considering the depth behind creating a system in your class or a program that supports Advanced Placement. Not to mention, the commitment to forming a relationship with every student will require as much work as a case manager compiling an IEP and, in many cases, involve just as much stress and frustration.

But let me offer you solace in explaining how much power you have to create your own success stories.

If you are fortunate enough to work in a district like mine, you understand how and why the district invests in your success as a teacher. When I received my AP assignment, the district offered to send me to a week-long College Board workshop to learn about the course from a veteran teacher. Many teachers who engage in this type of professional development say that it was the most comprehensive training they received in their entire graduate or undergraduate careers. The training focuses on content and skills but feels more like a combination of a history/methods class from college. The offer was on the table for me to take the train to Northwestern University for an entire week to prepare myself.

Just like we try to show the students how much we are invested in their success, my district was about to make a $1,000 deposit into my potential as an AP teacher. There was only one problem: I wasn't ready to make that investment myself. What if the district invested the time and money to prepare me, and the students still performed poorly? That certainly would single out my deficiencies as a teacher. It sure would validate some of the concerns of my colleagues when this all began.

You cannot teach in the "woulds." Not the w-o-o-d-s, but the "woulds."

These are the "woulds" in which I live, even today. *I wish I would have given more effort to my AP classes when I was in high school. I wish I would have paid more attention to academics and not sports. If I only would have invested more in my own professional development as a teacher.*

You cannot live life in the "woulds," which is to say: You cannot regret the opportunities placed in front of you—and cannot miss the opportunities you must make for you and your students.

I know what some of you must be thinking: *How can I be the difference when my students don't even know the difference between "analyze" and "explain" as a writing prompt?*

And I know what some of you must be feeling—the burden of responsibility on your shoulders as you lead students through this high-stakes journey.

I know what some of you must be saying, "It must be easy for you to say, *having done this already!*"

If nothing else, we know that it can be done. And you are precisely the person to do it.

Above professional development, strong vertical and horizontal curriculum, beyond having students with incredible talent and skills, or supportive administration and parents, *you* are the single greatest factor determining whether students will succeed in your class. You must be willing to make the investment in yourself or accept the investment that others are making in you. *Bet on yourself. Believe in yourself.* Creating a culture of success starts with you and your willingness to do things differently.

> ## Creating a culture of success starts with you and your willingness to do things differently.

If that seems isolating, understand that there is an entire AP community around you that is willing to help. As the saying goes, "There are four kinds of people in your life—those who add, multiply, subtract, and divide." The AP community will add to *and* multiply your professional circle. While we represent your students' competition on test day, we stand for something so much bigger than that. We want all of our students to succeed, and we want all of your students to succeed. Because, after all, "We got you."

As a high-schooler, around the time I was slogging my way through AP US History only to receive a 2 on the exam, my mother was putting her finishing touches on raising this teenage boy. Many of us could recall the parenting priorities our moms revealed over the years. My mom would insist on things like thank you cards, appropriate dress in public, and getting along with my sister. Those were priorities, but I remember more basic stuff too. Specifically, I remember my mother telling me to never get in a stranger's car and never talk to strangers on the internet.

Almost two decades later, I find myself using Uber to literally summon strangers to come and find me, so they can drive me wherever I want to go.

While my mother's advice is still wise, my point is that times have changed. Have you?

Like my friend at the conference who used this system to increase pass rates by 33 percent, take these ideas and begin your journey to reinvent your AP program or classroom. Perhaps you are already engaged in many of these practices and wish to push further. Use what you need and launch your students over the top. The stories of my students' successes are what you will probably remember, but don't forget that most of them worked within the SCORES system. Using the system, each teacher can make autonomous decisions that best fit his or her class or his or her style.

Never forget that you are the one who can be the difference. Embrace professional development when it is offered. Talk to your principal about making this initiative real. Walk into class tomorrow with a brand-new quiz policy. Have a "moment" with the most difficult student in your class. Meet the kids at the library at 8:00 p.m. on a Thursday night. Admit ownership in your scores. Believe in the power of writing conferences. Organize your own AP team. Email me with your questions and, most of all, don't live life in the "woulds."

I hope this book is the beginning of your story.

AFTERWORD

Mr. Sharos started writing this book during my junior year in high school. Our class accomplished something that had never been done before in the history of our school, and I think that surprised a lot of people. The success story of our class showed the administration, the younger generation of students, and the "haters" what we were *really* capable of. And, more importantly, it showed what our *community* was capable of.

I'll let you in on a secret: My mom worked in the dean's office at our school. She would often come home and mention the gossip she heard around the school the following year. While receiving much deserved praise, many teachers voiced their opinions on Mr. Sharos's enthusiastic approach to teaching and their opinions on why we did so well.

"Our school *never* scored that high on AP tests. It was just a fluke."

"He's so young; he can't do it again."

"He got lucky. He had the best students, and they were brighter and more motivated than mine."

After reading this book, you now know that Mr. Sharos's future classes shattered our record every subsequent year and competed with the highest-performing schools in the state. Rest assured, this was not just an anomaly.

I studied chemistry in college, and one of the first modes of thinking we were forced to adopt was the scientific method. *To prove or disprove a hypothesis, change the variable.* Having been in the trenches, let's apply this to my class that year. No AP class had achieved test scores higher than our APUSH class. And yet, the same group of students took other AP classes with the same stress and workload that came with it. But APUSH was the most daunting of them all, and our entire class dominated that test. What's the variable?

Looking back, I remember the culture of the class most. Our class embraced it and left a legacy in its wake. There's a certain necessity about doing well in AP classes, and the reward can sometimes bring out the best, or worst, in your students. Without a guide or a leader, we wouldn't have felt that necessity. Instead of competing for AP credit *against* one another, we competed *alongside* one another—a strong nod to the culture created by Mr. Sharos.

How can you create the culture your students need to succeed?

As a high school teacher, you have the amazing opportunity to change someone's life. Don't take that opportunity lightly. You can erase a past ridden with failure or self-doubt and shift your students toward a new future—a future filled with self-confidence and success. This book offers a process to do precisely that. I am one example of how adopting a new culture, perhaps a "one team, one dream" mentality, can bring about positive change to a student's path. As the saying goes, "It takes a village," and "it" begins with you.

I am not the only student of Mr. Sharos's that has gone on toward a better path, and I am privileged to have been a part of the journey. If you believe in the process and the system, embrace it and make it yours. I give you my word: Your students will follow.

I did. And, more importantly, we did.

—**Justin Thomas**

FREQUENTLY ASKED QUESTIONS

I am fortunate to travel the country and work with many different groups of teachers. Whether people hear a keynote speech, a conference session, or participate in a professional development day with me, I am often asked these questions about AP. I've included some of the questions, as well as my answers, in the pages that follow.

How many students did you have, and did they all take the test?

I hear this question a lot, especially from those of you who teach large sections of students in schools that have open enrollment policies. My smallest AP class ever was twenty-two students, and my largest was thirty. College Board recommends class sizes of seventeen for AP, so I was well above the recommendation. My school also had open enrollment, meaning that students could select AP classes even if they were not recommended for them. In each of the years I taught AP, I had one or two students drop my class at semester. However, every student took the exam at the end of the year.

How do the students at your school perform on AP tests overall?

Two years before I began teaching AP, our school-wide pass rate was 46 percent. By my final year of teaching AP, our school-wide pass rate was 72 percent. We did make some positive deposits in changing the culture of success of the program. However, the enrollment numbers were stagnant between 140–170 students taking at least one AP class. Three years after I left the classroom, over 300 students took the test and passed at a rate of 64 percent. This was a huge "win" for our school, considering so many more students were now a part of the program. We score above the state and national averages, even though we have never scored above state or national averages on ACT or SAT. Simply put, our AP program outperforms the expected outcomes of our students.

How do you handle students who want to drop your class?

This can happen from time to time when students are overwhelmed or face pressures outside of school. In the case of my students who dropped the class (a total of five over the years), factors beyond the classroom definitely contributed to their decision. Remember, students will hit "walls" throughout the year. Some students may feel overwhelmed early in the year, and it is our responsibility to help them fight through it instead of giving up. Academically, we have to wait until the end of the third unit or so to even consider dropping a student. The first unit can be a culture shock. The second unit is about recommending some adjustments. The third unit is about seeing if those adjustments are actually working. Give it some time.

What are your thoughts on dual credit classes with local colleges?

Many schools are struggling to enroll the "right" students in their AP or IB program because local colleges are offering dual credit classes. I support dual credit programs, especially for students who will struggle to pay for four to five years of higher education. However, my standard line is, "Dual credit means college credit, but AP means college readiness *and* college credit." In this case, we have to value the experience of AP, knowing data support systems that even a 2 on the exam increases chances of college completion exponentially. We know these dual credit courses are not as rigorous. Why not gain exposure to college-level readiness and earn credit in the process? Continue to advertise the advantages of AP to students beyond just receiving credit.

How did you handle summer homework?

Some schools have a policy that summer homework is not allowed because they do not want to punish transfer students or hold students accountable for work over the summer with a grade assigned during the school year. I understand both sides. I am a proponent of summer homework as a way to get a head start on the competition. The score assigned to the work does not have to be impactful to the larger grade in the course. I required the students to watch three movies from different historical periods in American history and create a colonial brochure to visit the New Americas. Most students would complete the work and at least establish a base for which to jump into chapter one. Be careful not to intimidate students with the rigor of your course. You can always wait until you begin to establish relationships and culture during the school year for more rigorous expectations.

How do you approach staffing your AP classes?

I speak to school leaders about this one frequently. AP teachers are often the best teachers in the school. But when this is not the case, many school administrators struggle with the extremes. Either the school has a ton of veteran teachers who feel entitled to teach "the good kids," or they have a vacuum of teachers who are willing to embrace the pressure of AP. I began teaching AP classes because of the latter reason. When I look at the totality of AP teachers, however, most of them are veterans who have paid their dues and have earned the right to teach these classes. But what if the teachers at this stage of their career are not giving their students the best effort? What if they are just poor teachers? What if they have lost the energy to challenge their students? This happens.

In administration and leadership, there is a fine line between crazy and courageous, and you have to flirt with it. You might be crazy if you completely remove a veteran teacher who has not played well in the sandbox and consistently underperforms his colleagues' scores. The withdrawals you make in the culture of your school and with your staff won't be worth it, especially if that teacher is well-respected among their peers. However, you can be courageous by giving a few sections away to a promising younger member of your staff. Start the process by transitioning sections away from the poor teacher and into the hands of the go-getter. If your institution and your gut feeling are correct, the data will validate your decision, and the proof will be in the pudding. As we know, the teacher makes a major difference. Your approach to staffing must be strategic and grounded in the philosophy of "what's best for kids."

How do you judge the success or failure of an AP teacher?

Our student enrollment in the AP program has doubled in the last four years. Remarkably, the pass rate on AP exams has remained relatively the same, going down just a few percentage points. Thus, the pass rate may be a tad lower, but the number of students who are passing at least one exam has skyrocketed. We want to celebrate the latter over the former. Teachers want to know that we value the number of students passing over the percentage of students passing, largely because the identification and outreach process will be focused on those "bubble" students.

When looking at individual teachers' sections, I always look to see if any of their students received a 5. Several years ago, we had a student score a perfect 36 on the ACT, and he attempted to take an AP test without taking the course. He independently studied AP Human Geography and attempted the exam in May. He received a 4, and he may have been one of the smartest, best test-takers we have ever seen.

That said, I believe it takes a teacher to help a student reach a 5. Most AP teachers will teach some of the smartest and most dedicated students in the school. Those students can probably score a 4 without you. But if students can score a 5, you know the teacher played a huge role in the outcome.

I am a new AP teacher–where do I start?

Over the summer, try to get to some professional development and work with other AP teachers. You have to start to create a network of other teachers to rely on. During my first summer, I spent time with the former APUSH teacher and the teacher at our other district school. In addition, I began to read the textbook, so I could understand how the reading schedule would flow during the year. Start to build your confidence by surrounding yourself with good people who take AP seriously. Try to use the SCORES system to ensure that your students understand the importance of the course. Once the class begins, focus on relationships and earning the trust of your students. You will be amazed at what your kids will do for you once they trust you.

I am a school leader who wants to reinvent our program–where do I start?

As a consultant, the most critical step we take in working with schools is listening. We cannot afford to listen *to reply*; we have to listen *to understand*. If you are an AP coordinator or a principal, consider sitting down with every stakeholder, one-on-one, to gather feedback on the "state of the union" in your AP program. Try not to make any decisions or determine a direction before you listen carefully to your staff and your students. Once you gather this information, commit to an active role in the turnaround process. We spoke about this earlier, but our principal takes an active role in every AP meeting. Our AP coordinator and counselor, Javier Vasquez, communicates well with our AP teachers and listens to their needs for how he can support a larger vision of AP in our school. This is not profound advice, but it is practical and will certainly be appreciated by your staff.

How does the "sign" campaign work?

We've used a website for the past five years to order our signs. Since the sign initiative gained so much attention on social media, over thirty different schools have reached out to us about the process. Some of them have found much cheaper options and still accomplished the same goal. Once we receive a list of students who received a 5, teachers deliver the signs right before the school year begins. On average, we deliver forty signs. However, in the spring, we give a different sign to every first-time AP student. Last year, we delivered over 270 signs as an acknowledgement of the courage it takes to enroll in AP.

Who should be on the "AP team?"

It might be best to start with who serves on our AP team. We have five AP teachers, five general education teachers, one special education teacher, two counselors, one AP coordinator, our director of community outreach, both assistant principals, and the principal. Covering all the stakeholders within the school is step one. Step two involves filling those roles with staff members who are positive and who are willing to put in extra time to help the program. The AP team is responsible for driving one of the most visible initiatives in the school. We are lucky to have members who command the respect of the rest of the faculty and who are willing to deliver a positive message about our process. When forming your team, these are a few of the folks you might look for, regardless of their role in the building:

1. The best teacher in the building
2. The biggest "kid" magnet on staff

3. The teacher who knows the most kids (usually a PE teacher or coach)

We also want a few staff members who are analytical. Sheer negativity has the potential to ruin the chemistry of the group, but it is valuable to invite a few teachers who are willing to examine the group's decisions with a critical eye.

25 CLASSROOM STRATEGIES

1. **Host writing conferences instead of grading major assignments by hand.**
   When I asked students what they remembered most about the class, they would often say, "Writing conferences." The best feedback is personal. At minimum, grade two assignments per year in a ten-minute, face-to-face conference (Chapter 2).

2. **Encourage test corrections for extra credit.**
   Test corrections serve two purposes: 1) encouraging students to correct mistakes and 2) boosting grades from difficult exams (Chapter 3).

3. **Create cumulative tests with old test questions.**
   Our unit tests, labs, and projects should be as difficult or more difficult that the test at the end of the year. However, include review questions to ensure retention of content (Chapter 3).

4. **Give practice tests starting at the end of March.**
   This may seem like an early time to start reviewing. Students must feel the urgency of the exam date and spread out their dedicated study time. Typically, students would receive a study guide over spring break and take a full AP test as soon as they returned from break (Chapter 3).

5. **Expose students to writing samples from College Board's website.**

College Board's website is rich with resources and practice exams. Consider using writing samples and have students evaluate the samples based on a rubric. If the students can understand the mindset of the graders, they can give the graders a better product (Chapter 3).

6. **Take the tests with the students.**

Build empathy for students by taking your own exams. Students must see you as a partner in this work. Be willing to accept students scoring higher than you (Chapter 1).

7. **Give quizzes any day or every day.**

Students need to feel a healthy anxiety about the prospect of a quiz each day. This will help encourage homework completion (Chapter 2).

8. **Give open-note quizzes.**

This is a gift to students. It is a way for you to say thank you for continuing to follow the homework schedule with consistency. It will also help reinforce taking useful notes (Chapter 2).

9. **Give "blank page quizzes."**

Nothing says, "Did you read last night?" more than a blank page that they must fill in. Ask students to tell you everything they can remember from the homework or reading (Chapter 2).

10. **Invite college professors to give your students a different voice.**

Students need to learn from a variety of different sources. They will tire quickly of your voice and the assigned text. Give your students exposure to college level instruction while they are in high school (Chapter 5).

11. **Use technology to engage students in relevant learning tasks.**

Use the three-question checklist to determine whether or not technology is the right tool to achieve the learning objective (Chapter 5).

- Does technology enhance my chances of engaging students?
- Can the students achieve an outcome only possible by using technology?
- Does technology streamline efficiency and still achieve the same outcome?

12. **Never assign anything that doesn't explicitly prepare students for the exam.**

This is a student-centered homework policy. Enter into a pact with your students promising to never assign busywork or enrichment that does not explicitly prepare them for the exam (Chapter 2).

13. **Give extra credit for anything that relates to preparing for the exam.**

If students are willing to do additional work and spend additional time preparing for the exam, we should reward the effort (Chapter 2).

14. **Place a strong emphasis on the test score, not the grade in the class.**

The more a teacher focuses on the grade, the more the students will focus on the grade. They already focus enough on the grade—steer them toward the larger goal of passing the national exam (Chapter 1).

15. **Be willing to revise policy or practice (confessions).**

    Approach your class with a degree of humility, knowing it is never too late to revise something. Your students look to you to model how to handle mistakes (Chapter 6).

16. **Flex your test and project schedule around other classes.**

    Everyone wins when teachers are flexible about when they give larger assessments or projects. Listen to the students and adjust accordingly (Chapter 4).

17. **Expose students to dozens of practice tests.**

    Taking practice tests is one of the best lessons you can plan. They first have to be equipped with the knowledge to attempt the test, but if students are comfortable with every portion of test, chances are they will carry that confidence into their performance (Chapter 3).

18. **Treat each student relationship like an IEP; be intentional about relationships.**

    Teachers should have a moment with every student during the year through a conversation, note, or exchange inside or outside of class. Make sure every student knows you care about their individual success (Chapter 4).

19. **Find the class leader and prioritize that relationship as a means to bring others into your culture.**

    The class leader has the ability to encourage other students to follow your system. Prioritize this relationship, knowing it could be the gateway to reaching the others (Chapter 4).

20. Match the commitment level you expect from your students.

"If you a run through a wall for me, I will run through a wall for you." Model this by committing deeply to your students' journey in AP. The students must see your efforts as a projection of what you expect from them in return (Chapter 6).

21. Use the words "however and because" in argumentative writing.

These two simple words ensure that each argument is layered with complexity. *However* implies the existence of a counter-claim, and *because* forces students to justify their argument (Chapter 2).

22. Set a tone that the AP class is different, with a higher purpose.

Treat the class differently. The students are not enrolled in an elective course; they are enrolled in Advanced Placement. Make sure students are aware of the opportunities they have through AP (Chapter 1).

23. Host practice test sessions after school and on Saturdays.

Teachers must buy as much time with their students as possible. It is a lot of work, but the sacrifice of Saturdays helps us gain ground on the competition (Chapter 5).

24. Allow make-up work for the purpose of mastery learning.

What is more important—a student's grade in the class or his or her mastery of the content and skills? This relates to the policy of offering extra credit. Allow students to continue working toward the larger goal, while putting less emphasis on their grade (Chapter 3).

25. **Do not preoccupy your time trying to catch cheating.**

    AP students cheat. Create a classroom culture where the cheaters only cheat themselves. The one person they won't be able to fool is the AP test grader (Chapter 2).

25 PROGRAM STRATEGIES

(For further explanation, see Chapter 7)

1. **Form an AP team.**

   This is number one on the list for a reason. The team serves as the guardians of the AP identification, outreach, and support process.

2. **Survey students about attributes that could lead to AP success.**

   Data-driven decision making is a powerful tool to leverage against folks in the building who do not believe in this work. Show them the data—especially the recommendations of staff members who stand behind a student's AP potential.

3. **The principal should lead the student identification process.**

   It is important for the initiative to be led by the instructional leader of the building. School leaders should see the power in the AP program's ability to change the entire school culture.

4. **Use measures like AP potential reports and GPA in identifying students for AP.**

   College Board gives us this data. We have to use it. Standardized test data helps determine readiness. The GPA is an indicator of work ethic. Both are important.

5. **Include AP team members from non-AP classes (PE, Special Education, etc.).**

   All voices should be valued in your space. PE teachers usually know a ton of students and can speak to students' soft skills like grit and determination. SPED teachers provide a unique perspective on learning styles.

6. **Allow time for AP teachers to collaborate across disciplines.**

   AP teachers should have their own professional learning community (PLC). We tend to think of curriculum groups through content areas. Why not organize a cross-curricular AP PLC?

7. **Have teachers articulate their AP tests to their department and other AP teachers.**

   It is very possible that your history teachers have never seen the science tests. There is value to this, and teachers will discover more commonalities than differences.

8. **Host a roundtable discussion with current AP students about the program.**

   Back to the idea of design thinking, we have to constantly check the pulse of our students.

9. **Create a summer program to build culture.**

   This is the hallmark of our support systems that are focused on growth mindset, AP habits of mind, and building unity among first-time AP students.

10. **Create an additional summer program for writing.**

    There is room for academic support in the summer. Do not overload the students with a six-week academic boot camp but offer writing support that crosses over different curricular areas.

11. **Challenge AP-ready sophomores to take honors classes first, then AP classes.**

The foundation of the AP program is the lower-level honors classes. Start building capacity there and use their performance as a barometer of AP readiness.

12. **Give out T-shirts for everything.**

Because, *why not?* Kids love T-shirts, and it's great marketing for the program. Someone in our school wears a "We Are AP" shirt every day.

13. **Serve food for breakfast meetings or host BBQs before football games.**

Food helps bring folks together, especially kids. Many students hang around after school before the games in the fall. Why not break out some speakers, a few "bags" sets, and the grills to provide a fun event for the kids?

14. **Promote passionate, younger staff to teach a few sections of AP if possible.**

We should staff our AP program with teachers who truly want to chase good scores and positive student outcomes, not teachers we are rewarding for longevity of service.

15. **Use yard signs to acknowledge students who received a 5.**

Hopefully the idea speaks for itself. We cannot go wrong by acknowledging the accomplishments of our students, validating the investments of the parents, and showing the community some awesome things happening inside our walls.

16. **Use yard signs to acknowledge first-time AP students.**

    This can be an expensive endeavor but a worthwhile one. Every student who attempts an AP class is taking a risk on themselves. Let's encourage that risk.

17. **Focus on the volume of passing scores, not the percentage of passing scores.**

    Teachers worry about pass rates. It is a good measure of success, but the best measure of success is how many *total* students passed the exam.

18. **Use social media to celebrate program and individual successes.**

    The word spreads quickly with every retweet, share, like, and forward. Use this strategy to help generate positive PR and marketing for the program.

19. **Send teachers to content-rich professional development from College Board.**

    College Board offers some wonderful resources and professional development. It will help encourage an AP mindset with your teachers and connect them to others in the field.

20. **Employ design-thinking to create support systems for students.**

    Ask students what they want. They are the end users of our product, so let them do some designing along the way.

21. **Develop an open enrollment policy.**

    Most schools have done this. Beyond adopting it, believe in what it stands for. Try to articulate as much about your program as you can. In this way, students will know exactly what they are signing up for and this may reduce requests to drop the class once they enroll.

22. Use staff feedback about students during the identification process.

One roadblock we often face is teacher resistance toward administration pushing AP. Give teachers a voice in the process.

23. Host bilingual parent nights to focus just on AP.

Give as much information to parents as possible. It is important that parents understand the expectations in AP and how they can support their students along the way. Their partnership will make all the difference. This is also a great opportunity to speak to parents about grades in AP and how they often correlate with the difficulty of the class.

24. Bring back former AP students to speak on panels for prospective students.

Any message delivered *by* students *to* students has power and agency. Encourage graduates to return to the school to interact with your current students. Most of your students will be thankful for this opportunity. Our prospective AP students continually acknowledge how much they enjoy hearing from their peers.

25. Create a video that recruits students for the AP program.

Using multimedia is crucial in putting a "face" on the program. A video tells a good story about the who, what, where, and, most importantly, the why of AP.

PLC AND BOOK STUDY RESOURCES

The SCORES System Review
Simplify homework
Create a quiz culture
Offer writing conferences
Review early and often
Evaluate cumulatively
Stop your agenda

The first three beliefs relate directly to logistics of classroom policy while the second three focus more on teacher philosophy.

Questions for Group Conversation or a Book Study

1. Compare and contrast your current system with the SCORES system. Where is there opportunity to integrate SCORES into your current practice?

2. Andrew lists several common excuses about test scores. Which one is the most prevalent in your school and how can you work to change it?

3. Based on standardized test data and the availability of additional resources, Andrew's students should not have performed as well on the AP test as they did. What do you think is the biggest reason that drove their success?

4. How can we be intentional about building relationships with the students we work with?

5. How can you use the success of the "Village Project" to promote a better identification and outreach process in your space?

6. What are the most important factors that impact the success of an AP team? What could this group look like at your school?

7. An AP program must include support systems for students and teachers. Which support systems mentioned may be the most impactful and why?

8. AP teachers rarely experience professional development and conversation together. How can we facilitate this conversation to make our vertical and horizontal instruction stronger?

9. What role does the administration play in supporting your AP program? Where is there room for growth at your school?

10. Which "student story" in the book best personifies the students you work with and why?

11. Which quote resonates with you most? How does it impact the way you teach and lead?

12. Find a quote or line from the book that you disagree with. Explain your pushback.

13. If Andrew taught in your school, what would be the biggest difference he would experience?

14. What questions do you have about the book that were not answered?

15. Do you believe that every student can pass an AP test if properly supported? Why or why not?

ACKNOWLEDGMENTS

I've wanted to tell my students' story for several years now, and this could not have happened without the help of many people.

I am so thankful to have found a publisher who is willing to share this message. To Shelley, Dave, Erin, and their entire team: "It was love at first sight." Thank you for seeing the soul in this story and for believing that it will make a difference for teachers, school leaders, and the students with whom they serve.

I feel completely humbled reading the foreword and afterword to this book. Andrew, thank you for your guidance, partnership, and friendship. Justin, you were my "once-in-a-career" student. Thank you for being a leader and convincing others to follow you.

To everyone who helped me write and edit, including my Dad, David Sharos (forever the best writer in our family): I appreciate your time, energy, and honesty.

To my principals, Wil and Tatiana, the two toughest people I know: Thank you for giving me a chance as a teacher and administrator. I'm in a career-long struggle to live up to the example you've set.

To my wife and best friend, Lizzie, and our two boys: Thank you always for supporting Dad's work.

And finally, to my former students: Thank you for running through a wall for me. Moreover, I am proud that your accomplishments will inspire others for years to come. This is our story, but you are the true heroes.

MORE FROM
DAVE BURGESS
Consulting, Inc.

Teach Like a PIRATE

Increase Student Engagement, Boost Your Creativity, and Transform Your Life as an Educator

By Dave Burgess (@BurgessDave)

New York Times' bestseller *Teach Like a PIRATE* sparked a worldwide educational revolution with its passionate teaching manifesto and dynamic student-engagement strategies. Translated into multiple languages, it sparks outrageously creative lessons and life-changing student experiences.

P is for PIRATE

Inspirational ABC's for Educators

By Dave and Shelley Burgess (@Burgess_Shelley)

In *P is for Pirate*, husband-and-wife team Dave and Shelley Burgess tap personal experiences of seventy educators to inspire others to create fun and exciting places to learn. It's a wealth of imaginative and creative ideas that makes learning and teaching more fulfilling than ever before.

The Innovator's Mindset

Empower Learning, Unleash Talent, and Lead a Culture of Creativity

By George Couros (@gcouros)

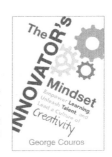

In *The Innovator's Mindset*, teachers and administrators discover that compliance to a scheduled curriculum hinders student innovation, critical thinking, and creativity. To become forward-thinking leaders, students must be empowered to wonder and explore.

Pure Genius

Building a Culture of Innovation and Taking 20% Time to the Next Level

By Don Wettrick (@DonWettrick)

Collaboration—with experts, students, and other educators—helps create interesting and even life-changing opportunities for learning. In *Pure Genius*, Don Wettrick inspires and equips educators with a systematic blueprint for beating classroom boredom and teaching innovation.

Learn Like a PIRATE

Empower Your Students to Collaborate, Lead, and Succeed

By Paul Solarz (@PaulSolarz)

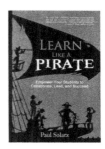

Passing grades don't equip students for life and career responsibilities. *Learn Like a PIRATE* shows how risk-taking and exploring passions in stimulating, motivating, supportive, self-directed classrooms creates students capable of making smart, responsible decisions on their own.

Ditch That Textbook

Free Your Teaching and Revolutionize Your Classroom

By Matt Miller (@jmattmiller)

Ditch That Textbook creates a support system, toolbox, and manifesto that can free teachers from outdated textbooks. Miller empowers them to untether themselves, throw out meaningless, pedestrian teaching and learning practices, and evolve and revolutionize their classrooms.

50 Things You Can Do with Google Classroom

By Alice Keeler and Libbi Miller
(@alicekeeler, @MillerLibbi)

50 Things You Can Do with Google Classroom provides a thorough overview of this GAfE app and shortens the teacher learning curve for introducing technology in the classroom. Keeler and Miller's ideas, instruction, and screenshots help teachers go digital with this powerful tool.

50 Things to Go Further with Google Classroom

A Student-Centered Approach

By Alice Keeler and Libbi Miller
(@alicekeeler, @MillerLibbi)

In *50 Things to Go Further with Google Classroom: A Student-Centered Approach*, authors and educators Alice Keeler and Libbi Miller help teachers create a digitally rich, engaging, student-centered environment that taps the power of individualized learning using Google Classroom.

140 Twitter Tips for Educators

Get Connected, Grow Your Professional Learning Network, and Reinvigorate Your Career

By Brad Currie, Billy Krakower, and Scott Rocco
(@bradmcurrie, @wkrakower, @ScottRRocco)

In *140 Twitter Tips for Educators*, #Satchat hosts and founders of Evolving Educators, Brad Currie, Billy Krakower, and Scott Rocco, offer step-by-step instruction on Twitter basics and building an online following within Twitter's vibrant network of educational professionals.

Master the Media

How Teaching Media Literacy Can Save Our Plugged-In World

By Julie Smith (@julnilsmith)

Master the Media explains media history, purpose, and messaging so teachers and parents can empower students with critical-thinking skills which lead to informed choices, the ability to differentiate between truth and lies, and discern perception from reality. Media literacy can save the world.

The Zen Teacher

Creating Focus, Simplicity, and Tranquility in the Classroom

By Dan Tricarico (@thezenteacher)

Unrushed and fully focused, teachers influence—even improve—the future when they maximize performance and improve their quality of life. In *The Zen Teacher*, Dan Tricarico offers practical, easy-to-use techniques to develop a non-religious Zen practice and thrive in the classroom.

eXPlore Like a Pirate

*Gamification and Game-Inspired Course Design to Engage,
Enrich, and Elevate Your Learners*

By Michael Matera (@MrMatera)

Create an experiential, collaborative, and creative world
with classroom game designer and educator Michael Matera's
game-based learning book, *eXPlore Like a Pirate*. Matera
helps teachers apply motivational gameplay techniques and
enhance curriculum with gamification strategies.

Your School Rocks . . . So Tell People!

*Passionately Pitch and Promote the Positives Happening
on Your Campus*

By Ryan McLane and Eric Lowe (@McLane_Ryan, @EricLowe21)

Your School Rocks . . . So Tell People! helps schools create
effective social media communication strategies that keep
students' families and the community connected to what's
going on at school, offering more than seventy immediately
actionable tips with easy-to-follow instructions and video
tutorial links.

Play Like a Pirate

Engage Students with Toys, Games, and Comics

By Quinn Rollins (@jedikermit)

In *Play Like a Pirate*, Quinn Rollins offers practical, engaging strategies and resources that make it easy to integrate fun
into your curriculum. Regardless of grade level, serious learning can be seriously fun with inspirational ideas that engage
students in unforgettable ways.

The Classroom Chef

*Sharpen Your Lessons. Season Your Classes. Make Math
Meaningful*

By John Stevens and Matt Vaudrey
(@Jstevens009, @MrVaudrey)

With imagination and preparation, every teacher can be
The Classroom Chef using John Stevens and Matt Vaudrey's
secret recipes, ingredients, and tips that help students "get"
math. Use ideas as-is, or tweak to create enticing educational
meals that engage students.

How Much Water Do We Have?

5 Success Principles for Conquering Any Challenge and Thriving in Times of Change

By Pete Nunweiler with Kris Nunweiler

Stressed out, overwhelmed, or uncertain at work or home? It could be figurative dehydration.

How Much Water Do We Have? identifies five key elements necessary for success of any goal, life transition, or challenge. Learn to find, acquire, and use the 5 Waters of Success.

The Writing on the Classroom Wall

How Posting Your Most Passionate Beliefs about Education Can Empower Your Students, Propel Your Growth, and Lead to a Lifetime of Learning

By Steve Wyborney (@SteveWyborney)

Big ideas lead to deeper learning, but they don't have to be profound to have profound impact. Teacher Steve Wyborney explains why and how sharing ideas sharpens and refines them. It's okay if some ideas fall off the wall; what matters most is sharing and discussing.

Kids Deserve It!

Pushing Boundaries and Challenging Conventional Thinking

By Todd Nesloney and Adam Welcome (@TechNinjaTodd, @awelcome)

Think big. Make learning fun and meaningful. *Kids Deserve It!* Nesloney and Welcome offer high-tech, high-touch, and highly engaging practices that inspire risk-taking and shake up the status quo on behalf of your students. Rediscover why you became an educator, too!

LAUNCH

Using Design Thinking to Boost Creativity and Bring Out the Maker in Every Student

By John Spencer and A.J. Juliani (@spencerideas, @ajjuliani)

When students identify themselves as makers, inventors, and creators, they discover powerful problem-solving and critical-thinking skills. Their imaginations and creativity will shape our future. John Spencer and A.J. Juliani's *LAUNCH* process dares you to innovate and empower them.

Instant Relevance

Using Today's Experiences to Teach Tomorrow's Lessons

By Denis Sheeran (@MathDenisNJ)

Learning sticks when it's relevant to students. In *Instant Relevance,* author and keynote speaker Denis Sheeran equips you to create engaging lessons *from* experiences and events that matter to students while helping them make meaningful connections between the real world and the classroom.

Escaping the School Leader's Dunk Tank

How to Prevail When Others Want to See You Drown

By Rebecca Coda and Rick Jetter
(@RebeccaCoda, @RickJetter)

Dunk-tank situations—discrimination, bad politics, revenge, or ego-driven coworkers—can make an educator's life miserable. Coda and Jetter (dunk-tank survivors themselves) share real-life stories and insightful research to equip school leaders with tools to survive and, better yet, avoid getting "dunked."

Start. Right. Now.

Teach and Lead for Excellence

By Todd Whitaker, Jeff Zoul, and Jimmy Casas
(@ToddWhitaker, @Jeff_Zoul, @casas_jimmy)

Excellent leaders and teachers *Know the Way, Show the Way, Go the Way, and Grow Each Day.* Whitaker, Zoul, and Casas share four key behaviors of excellence from educators across the U.S. and motivate to put you on the right path.

Lead Like a PIRATE

Make School Amazing for Your Students and Staff

By Shelley Burgess and Beth Houf
(@Burgess_Shelley, @BethHouf)

Lead Like a PIRATE maps out character traits necessary to captain a school or district. You'll learn where to find treasure already in your classrooms and schools—and bring out the best in educators. Find encouragement in your relentless quest to make school amazing for everyone!

Teaching Math with Google Apps

50 G Suite Activities

By Alice Keeler and Diana Herrington

(@AliceKeeler, @mathdiana)

 Teaching Math with Google Apps meshes the easy student/teacher interaction of Google Apps with G Suite that empowers student creativity and critical thinking. Keeler and Herrington demonstrate fifty ways to bring math classes into the twenty-first century with easy-to-use technology.

Table Talk Math

A Practical Guide for Bringing Math into Everyday Conversations

By John Stevens (@Jstevens009)

 In *Table Talk Math*, John Stevens offers parents—and teachers—ideas for initiating authentic, math-based, everyday conversations that get kids to notice and pique their curiosity about the numbers, patterns, and equations in the world around them.

Shift This!

How to Implement Gradual Change for Massive Impact in Your Classroom

By Joy Kirr (@JoyKirr)

 Establishing a student-led culture focused on individual responsibility and personalized learning *is* possible, sustainable, and even easy when it happens little by little. In *Shift This!*, Joy Kirr details gradual shifts in thinking, teaching, and approach for massive impact in your classroom.

Unmapped Potential

An Educator's Guide to Lasting Change

By Julie Hasson and Missy Lennard (@PPrincipals)

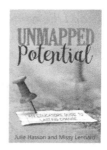

 Overwhelmed and overworked? You're not alone, but it can get better. You simply need the right map to guide you from frustrated to fulfilled. *Unmapped Potential* offers advice and practical strategies to forge a unique path to becoming the educator and *person* you want to be.

Shattering the Perfect Teacher Myth

6 Truths That Will Help You THRIVE as an Educator

By Aaron Hogan (@aaron_hogan)

Author and educator Aaron Hogan helps shatter the idyllic "perfect teacher" myth, which erodes self-confidence with unrealistic expectations and sets teachers up for failure. His book equips educators with strategies that help them shift out of survival mode and THRIVE.

Social LEADia

Moving Students from Digital Citizenship to Digital Leadership

By Jennifer Casa-Todd (@JCasaTodd)

A networked society requires students to leverage social media to connect to people, passions, and opportunities to grow and make a difference. *Social LEADia* helps shift focus at school and home from digital citizenship to digital leadership and equip students for the future.

Spark Learning

3 Keys to Embracing the Power of Student Curiosity

By Ramsey Musallam (@ramusallam)

Inspired by his popular TED Talk "3 Rules to Spark Learning," Musallam combines brain science research, proven teaching methods, and his personal story to empower you to improve your students' learning experiences by inspiring inquiry and harnessing its benefits.

Ditch That Homework

Practical Strategies to Help Make Homework Obsolete

By Matt Miller and Alice Keeler (@jmattmiller, @alicekeeler)

In *Ditch That Homework*, Miller and Keeler discuss the pros and cons of homework, why it's assigned, and what life could look like without it. They evaluate research, share parent and teacher insights, then make a convincing case for ditching it for effective and personalized learning methods.

The Four O'Clock Faculty

A Rogue Guide to Revolutionizing Professional Development

By Rich Czyz (@RACzyz)

In *The Four O'Clock Faculty*, Rich identifies ways to make professional learning meaningful, efficient, and, above all, personally relevant. It's a practical guide to revolutionize PD, revealing why some is so awful and what *you* can do to change the model for the betterment of everyone.

Culturize

Every Student. Every Day. Whatever It Takes.

By Jimmy Casas (@casas_jimmy)

Culturize dives into what it takes to cultivate a community of learners who embody innately human traits our world desperately needs—kindness, honesty, and compassion. Casas's stories reveal how "soft skills" can be honed while exceeding academic standards of twenty-first-century learning.

Code Breaker

Increase Creativity, Remix Assessment, and Develop a Class of Coder Ninjas!

By Brian Aspinall (@mraspinall)

You don't have to be a "computer geek" to use coding to turn curriculum expectations into student skills. Use *Code Breaker* to teach students how to identify problems, develop solutions, and use computational thinking to apply and demonstrate learning.

The Wild Card

7 Steps to an Educator's Creative Breakthrough

By Hope and Wade King (@hopekingteach, @wadeking7)

The Kings facilitate a creative breakthrough in the classroom with *The Wild Card*, a step-by-step guide to drawing on your authentic self to deliver your content creatively and be the *wild card* who changes the game for your learners.

Stories from Webb

The Ideas, Passions, and Convictions of a Principal and His School Family

By Todd Nesloney (@TechNinjaTodd)

Stories from Webb goes right to the heart of education. Told by award-winning principal Todd Nesloney and his dedicated team of staff and teachers, this book reminds you why you became an educator. Relatable stories reinvigorate and may inspire you to tell your own!

The Principled Principal

10 Principles for Leading Exceptional Schools

By Jeffrey Zoul and Anthony McConnell (@Jeff_Zou, @mcconnellaw)

Zoul and McConnell know from personal experience that the role of school principal is one of the most challenging *and* the most rewarding in education. Using relatable stories and real-life examples, they reveal ten core values that will empower you to work and lead with excellence.

The Limitless School

Creative Ways to Solve the Culture Puzzle

By Abe Hege and Adam Dovico (@abehege, @adamdovico)

Being intentional about creating a positive culture is imperative for your school's success. This book identifies the nine pillars that support a positive school culture and explains how each stakeholder has a vital role to play in the work of making schools safe, inviting, and dynamic.

Google Apps for Littles

Believe They Can

By Christine Pinto and Alice Keeler (@PintoBeanz11, @alicekeeler)

Learn how to tap into students' natural curiosity using technology. Pinto and Keeler share a wealth of innovative ways to integrate digital tools in the primary classroom to make learning engaging and relevant for even the youngest of today's twenty-first-century learners.

ABOUT THE AUTHOR

Andrew Sharos has spent his entire career at West Leyden High School, winner of College Board's AP District of the Year honors in 2014. He earned his undergraduate degree from Marquette University, his master's degree from Olivet Nazarene University, and his endorsement in School Business from Northern Illinois University.

Andrew has been a teacher, coach, and building administrator. He is the founder and CEO of the Village Project Consulting Group, which provides professional development to schools to improve their AP programs and their overall building culture. He has keynoted and presented at conferences across the country. Andrew has also authored two manuals with the Bureau of Education and Research, both focused on using technology and flipped classroom methods in social studies. In 2018, Andrew was named the winner of College Board's "Distinguished Service Award," given to a forceful spokesperson for important educational and societal goals.

Andrew has been married to his wife, Lizzie, since 2009. Instead of chasing AP test scores, he now chases their two toddlers, Cooper and Parker.

Contact Andrew

 AndrewSharos.com

 andrew.sharos@gmail.com

 @AndrewSharosAP

Made in the USA
Monee, IL
21 November 2020